THE REAL RIGHT RETURNS

In memory of Dominique Venner.

DANIEL FRIBERG

THE REAL
RIGHT
RETURNS

A HANDBOOK FOR THE TRUE OPPOSITION

ARKTOS

LONDON 2015

Printed in the United Kingdom.

ISBN 978-1-910524-49-7

BIC-CLASSIFICATION
Conservatism and right-of-centre democratic ideologies (JPFM)
Nationalism (JPFN)
Political science and theory (JPA)

EDITORS
Martin Locker
John B Morgan

ARKTOS MEDIA LTD.
www.arktos.com

Contents

Preface

Forging the True Right

The book you are currently reading is not written by someone who is only a theorist, but by someone who has had a great deal of experience in the trenches of Europe's New Right.

I first came into contact with my friend and colleague Daniel Friberg in 2009, at the time when I was still part of Arktos' predecessor, Integral Tradition Publishing, and we were in the planning stages of creating what was to become Arktos Media the following year. Being from the United States I hadn't known much about him at first, but as I got to know more about the New Right that had been emerging in Sweden over the previous decade, it quickly became apparent from my conversations with others that Daniel was one of, if not the, key figure in the creation of a vital, and vitally needed, New Right there. His devotion to the Swedish cause was apparent from the many years he had been involved with it, something which is quite remarkable in a frustrating milieu in which few have the patience to stick it out for more than a short time, as well as the sheer number of the various projects with which he had been active. This told me that here was a man who would have the dedication and perseverance needed to develop Arktos over the long-term, especially in its difficult and trying early years. Daniel amply demonstrated that this was the case during the time we were based in India, when comforts were few and just getting through everyday life often involved a great deal of struggle and hardship. (If you've ever tried to run an international business from India and then had to get tech support to help you when your Internet went down, you'll have some idea of the adventures we frequently had.) And fortunately, this paid off, given that Arktos is now over five years old and continues to grow and thrive.

Another fortunate aspect of our collaboration has been that Daniel and I have always seen eye-to-eye on the direction that Arktos should take; namely, introducing new ideas and perspectives into the Right in order to reinvigorate it, and experimenting with new and unorthodox methods for achieving this. The post-war Right throughout the West can be characterised in either of two ways: a gradual compromise with, and ultimate surrender to, the language, assumptions, and perspectives of the liberal Left; or a type of reactionary clinging to a vanished, and in some cases overly idealised, past which renders its adherents as nothing more than whiners shaking their fists at the world around them as they grow ever more out-of-touch with their own people and the times. With Arktos, we wanted to do our part to try to change the conversation on the Right, both by attempting to alter the foundations of its discourse as well as by helping to find a new language and method with which to express its ideas.

While we have always agreed that Arktos should not try to promote any single ideology or system of beliefs, and should not even devote itself exclusively to works of a political nature, it is nevertheless the case that the idea of helping to allow the ideas of the New Right to reach a wider audience has been central to our conception of Arktos from the outset. The term 'New Right' is a frequently-used term these days which has come to be rather vague, given that there are so many different ideas about what, exactly, constitutes the New Right. For this reason I personally prefer the term 'true Right', which Julius Evola occasionally used. This type of Right is not 'conservative' in the usual understanding of the term, since it does not seek to preserve European civilisation as it is today or as it has been in the recent past. Rather, it attempts to reconstitute those ideals and values which were taken for granted in Europe prior to the advent of liberalism. Nor is the true Right even 'Right-wing' in the conventional sense. If we look back to the political, philosophical, and social worldview of the Holy Roman Empire or of Classical Athens, for example, we find a way of conceiving things that, to our modern minds, seems like something surprisingly new and challenging. It cannot be defined as Left or Right — but combines elements of both. To give an example, it cannot be denied that local communities in the medieval or ancient world had far more autonomy than they are granted in modern nation-states, for example; in many respects, then, the various regions which made up the Holy Roman Empire actually enjoyed more freedom and diversity than the countries which today make up the European Union or the states which comprise the US. Looking back before the world of liberalism therefore presents us with revolutionary ideas — especially when we remember that the original meaning of 'revolution' referred to returning something to its origins rather than to an attempt to bring about utopian change, as it usually means in relation to politics today.

At the same time, the moniker of 'New' is appropriate in some ways, given that we do not simply want to turn the clock back to an earlier time. The New Right is indeed new in that, while it engages with many ideas and concepts that are nearly forgotten, it is likewise willing to meet the modern world on its own terms, and looks for ways of integrating the best traditions and values of the past with contemporary developments in culture, philosophy, science, and society in general. Unlike Gatsby, we acknowledge that we cannot repeat the past, as glorious as it sometimes was. The world is forever changing, and with it the needs of societies and civilisations. We can look to the wisdom of our ancestors for guidance to help us navigate in this extremely complex and chaotic age, and indeed, it is our obligation to those who made it possible for us to exist that we do not neglect their memory or their legacy. But we should not allow that to make us afraid of change or of looking for potential in new ideas. We must in a sense be radical — not in order to bring about change for its own sake, but rather to find our place in the new historical paradigm into which we have been thrown. To accomplish this we should be willing to engage with whatever it takes, in any field or from any source, in order to figure out what the next steps of our civilisation should be. A case in point: technology is rapidly altering the way in which we work as well as how we understand the nature of identity, and any political force which wants to remain relevant in the future will have to have a clearly thought-out approach to these issues. Do we simply abandon the traditional conceptions of work and identity in favour of an uncertain future, or do we develop a new means for approaching them that is consistent with our beliefs? The Right must come to terms with this. Simply insisting that we stick to older ways of doing things that are no longer relevant, and which few people will respond to, is a recipe for failure.

Where the old and the new meet and are synthesised — this is the place which the New Right seeks to occupy, and the essays in this book are the product of Daniel's many years of grappling with the issues stemming from how we can accomplish this, both in thought and in action. He introduces the basic concepts of the New Right and some of its history, and offers advice on how to deal with the opposition. Even though it is becoming more obvious by the day that the majority of people in Europe and America are coming around to our point of view, there are those on the Left, and even in the useless faction which calls itself 'Right' in the political establishment, who sense their power beginning to slip, and try to demonise us by calling us names: 'fascist', 'Nazi', 'racist', and 'white supremacist' being among their favourites. As such, we have to be prepared in knowing how to respond. Daniel offers some cogent practical advice in this regard as well.

If you are new to the world of the New Right, welcome, and I hope this book offers you some food for thought as you begin your journey. If you find yourself agreeing with it, never stop reading and thinking, and get active in whatever way your talents and proclivities are most suited. The struggle is only just beginning, and it will grow to encompass every field of human activity in the coming years. And hopefully this book will also show you that, contrary to how it may sometimes seem, you are not alone.

JOHN B MORGAN
Editor-in-Chief, Arktos Media
Budapest, Hungary
30 September 2015

Foreword

Daniel Friberg and the Swedish Right

Ten years ago, the Swedish Right was at an impasse. The available options on the political stage were few, as the choice stood between a conservative Right already on its death bed (today, it has long since flat-lined), a moderate critique of immigration from a liberal perspective, and the nationalist movement. Each of these options had its limitations. The most commonly chosen option, the liberal critique, lacked an acknowledgment of the positive and genuine significance of ethnic differences, and was marked by its opposition to any broader historical perspective. The absence of a genuine, consistent Right possessing robust ideas, uncorrupted by a pragmatic adaptation to the doctrines of the radical Leftist elites, was painfully obvious.

This Gordian knot was cut largely by the author of the book you are currently holding. This provides a valuable lesson in metapolitics in and of itself, a crash course in how to analyse supply and demand on the political market. As far as demand is concerned, metapolitics concerns itself, among other things, with identifying those groups which exist in a given society, and which such groups lack political and ideological representation. In Sweden, as in all of Europe, this would be the large majority of John and Jane Does. The primary metapolitical task, then, is to make this group conscious of the general state of affairs, and of their own actual and legitimate interests. They must also be reminded of the fact that Swedes and Europeans exist, that they have a history, have justified claims and interests, and possess a culture which is their own.

Just as important, but more difficult, is the supply side — to analyse the available ideological and political milieus, and if necessary to change them, or even to increase their number. The solution to the problem of breaking the Swedish impasse, it was suggested, is to introduce and adapt the school of thought which is known as the European New Right. That this would succeed was far from certain. This task demanded individuals with con-siderable intellectual resources, determination, and strength of will, as well as a combination of pragmatism, political instinct, and vision. Daniel Friberg was one such individual, and it is extremely debatable whether there would have been a Swedish New Right without him. This makes it especially interesting to investigate his political thinking.

The New Right, which began in France under the auspices of Alain de Benoist and his GRECE (*Groupement de Recherche et d'Études pour la Civilisation Européenne*) organisation, originally acquired its name against its will in the 1970s, having been baptised thusly by the French media establishment. The debate still rages over whether our ideas constitute the latest incarnation of the true Right, or if they stand 'beyond Left and Right'. There are cases to be made for either position, but in order to describe our ideas as beyond Left and Right, one must accept the present definition of what 'the Right' is. What is today portrayed as 'the Right' is, in fact, an imposter. It is easy to recognise, with its rhetorical focus on 'the market', its fixation on 'individualism' and 'freedom', its Atlanticist loyalty to Brussels and the White House, and its apathy or hostility towards any conception of European identities, values, and traditions. If this 'false Right' is contrasted with the 'true Right', one will find within the latter strains which might be described as 'socialist', with a focus on solidarity within organic groups, but also strains which might be viewed as 'liberal' (in the European sense, *nota bene*), with a strong focus on liberties. When compared to these ideas, those of Swedish and European 'conservative parties' stand out as merely pretend Rightists.

In Sweden, and perhaps elsewhere, there is ample reason for the opposition to embrace the genuine 'Right wing' concept, since it has been largely abandoned by the political forces that used to defend it. Its use clearly illustrates the fact that we are not a part of the 'Establishment', but in fact we are its only true challengers. In the history of our ideas, we find a complete alternative in terms of a worldview, an approach to history, social ideals, and anthropology in the New Right. Anthropology in particular should come to play an increasing part in the coming years, since, given that the *de facto* ideal man of the official Western ideology is a snack-munching couch potato, our alternative will come to be seen as one which is more attractive all the time. The ideas of 1789 have reached the end of their road, and today the consequences they have had for society as well as the individuals that constitute it have become painfully obvious. The alternative is the New Right, whose ideas the author of this book is especially qualified to present.

JOAKIM ANDERSEN
Co-Editor, *Motpol*

1

The Return of the Real Right

The Left's cultural dominion, which lasted from 1945 until 1989, is over. The consensus that existed between Communists, Christian Democrats, and the Socialists after the Second World War is gone. The taboos have been shattered — forever.

— GÁSPÁR MIKLÓS TAMÁS

After more than half a century of retreat, marginalisation, and constant concessions to an ever-more aggressive and demanding Left, the true European Right is returning with a vengeance. This is happening not a day too soon; Europe faces a long list of problems, not to mention threats. There is no question of the Left or the liberal Right possessing the will or the ability to solve these problems — indeed, they are the two main problems. The return of the ideas of the traditional Right is, indeed, something that concerns us all.

The Left's Cultural War of Conquest

As late as the 1950s, traditional ideals were considered the norm in most of Europe. The nuclear family was regarded as the basic foundation of society and the relatively homogeneous ethnic composition of the European nations was not seen as a problem to be solved by mass immigration. Today, more than 60 years later, the ideals of the West have been completely inverted, and ideas that originally belonged to the periphery of the extreme Left have been elevated to social norms that today dominate the education sector, the media, our government institutions, and private NGOs.

In his excellent book, *New Culture, New Right*,[1] Michael O'Meara presents the path of development that brought us to this point. One of the factors he addresses is the Frankfurt School and its concept of Critical Theory. Marxist sociologists and philosophers at the Frankfurt *Institut fur Sozialforschung* in the early twentieth century aimed, through their conception of philosophy and selective social analysis, to undermine confidence in traditional values and hierarchies. Its ambitions were to play, through a process that is too complex to account for in this short piece, an increasingly significant role in the post-war period.

---

1   *New Culture, New Right: Anti-Liberalism in Postmodern Europe* (London: Arktos, 2013).

Many of the Frankfurt School's ideas are prevalent in both the Left's and the media's description of reality today. In a society characterised by uncontrolled immigration and related social problems, they try to convince their populations that the crucial factor is Western racism. The concepts of a 'right to birth control' and radical feminism seem tailor-made to maximise the selfishness of both genders, as well as to reduce the number of births to well below replacement level; 'patriarchy' and 'traditional gender roles' are regarded as if they were harmful concepts in public debate.

Mass immigration, sexual liberalism, and many other negative political and cultural choices cannot be fully explained by the activities of Leftist politicians alone. Without the Frankfurt School and similar projects it is unlikely, if not inconceivable, that they would have taken the shapes they did. In order to understand how one of history's greatest civilisations — in what could be seen as a brief moment in terms of historical time — has undergone a drastic transformation from a life-affirming to a genuinely self-destructive social form, one needs an understanding of the role of metapolitics in the social upheavals of the latter part of the twentieth century.

The concept of metapolitics was developed by the Italian Communist Antonio Gramsci in his quest to analyse the reasons behind the fact that the Communist revolution never succeeded in Western Europe. According to Gramsci, this was because the bourgeois cultural hegemony had to be broken first in order to make society receptive to the idea of a Communist takeover. Guided by this analysis, the Left later began what a German Leftist termed their *long march through the institutions,* and finally secured Leftist cultural hegemony in Europe—a hegemony that was achieved through a long-term, persistent, and uncompromising meta-policy. Neither political violence nor parliamentary politics played a major role in this process, even if it came to influence both. The result was indeed different than Gramsci would have imagined, as has been discussed by Paul Gottfried in *The Strange Death of Marxism,*[2] but a result certainly came about.

Metapolitics can be defined as the process of disseminating and anchoring a particular set of cultural ideas, attitudes, and values in a society, which eventually leads to deeper political change. This work need not—and perhaps should not—be linked to a particular party or programme. The point is ultimately to redefine *the conditions under which politics is conceived,* which the European cultural Left pushed to its extreme. The metapolitical chokehold that political correctness has over Western Europe is a result of consistent cultivation—or rather misuse—of this strategy. Only by understanding this tool, countering its misuse, and turning it to serve our own ends, can we overcome the miserable situation that our continent is in.

---

2   *The Strange Death of Marxism: The European Left in the New Millennium* (Columbia, Missouri: University of Missouri Press, 2005).

The Fall of the Old Right

The Left's advance during the second half of the twentieth century was made possible by three main factors:

1. After the Second World War, the Right was associated with the losing side, most especially Nazism. The fact that concentration camps and systematic political persecution were prevalent to the same degree, if not more so, in the victorious Soviet Union, as it had been in the earlier French Revolution which first gave rise to liberalism, was much more effectively dealt with by the revolutionary Left than the reactionary Right, as the Left's apologists managed to effectively sweep all of these crimes under the carpet.

2. The Left's aforementioned long march through the institutions escalated during the '60s and '70s, and culminated in their usurpation of the media, cultural institutions, and educational systems — in other words those pillars of society which shape people's thoughts and opinions.

3. The Left which developed in Western Europe and North America under the guidance of figures such as Herbert Marcuse took on an eccentric shape. In this new form of the Left, the European working class was dismissed as incurably reactionary, and was replaced in its previous role as the revolutionary subject by sexual and ethnic minorities. This coincided with the rise of powerful, new economic and

political interests and tendencies in the West. The beliefs of Marcusian Leftism, where class struggle and economic redistribution was drowned out by a cult of the individual and strange forms of (minority) identity politics, were consistent with the concept of the ideal consumer developed by the oligarchs of the new global marketplace of liberalism. Likewise, the American government's determination to prevent its own domestic Leftist opposition from establishing anything friendly with the Soviet Union or otherwise politically effective made Marcusian Leftism an ideal fallback strategy.

The Left's successful metapolitics, in which decades of persistent struggle gradually managed to give it control over the vital culture-forming institutions, can certainly serve as an instructive example of what we now need to implement in pursuit of our own goals. At the same time, it is also a warning signal. To the extent that the Leftist project set out to create economic equality and end the alienation of the individual in modern society — in other words, what Marx had advocated — it has obviously failed miserably. Despite its firm grip on the public debate in Sweden (for example), in practice the Left achieves little more than to fill the role of global capitalism's court jester. Despite this, it continues to succeed in its other main goal, which has been to prevent Europe's native populations from defending themselves against a political project that undermines their right to political self-determination. Toward this end, sentimentality was substituted for Marxist historical analysis. Even its relatively limited forms of economic redistribution policies have been gradually relegated to the rubbish heap of history, except for the redistribution of financial resources from the European middle classes to both big business and the growing foreign *lumpenproletariat* which has been dumped on European soil. If today we refer to the spectre of Communism haunting Europe, as Marx claimed in his *Manifesto*, it is quite a truncated phantom of which we speak.

What this indicates is that the Left's advances have largely taken place with both the approval and impetus of the elites of the Western world, which is not something a genuine Rightist movement can count on. The Right, however, unlike the Left, have the advantage in that they are simply more correct on many issues. Our description of reality is more in line with what people actually experience in everyday life (which is of crucial importance in politics), and our predictions and explanatory methods are more consistent with what is actually happening in our communities. This is still no guarantee of success, but it is an advantage.

When we speak of the Right, it is important to be clear that we do not speak of the Left-liberal parody that currently goes by that name as in, for example, the Swedish public debate. The Swedish 'Right-wing', with its slip towards the Left and its inherent weakness and timidity, is unworthy of the name, just as with the Republicans in the United States or the Tories in Britain. The rise of this type of 'Right' in the post-war period is a direct consequence of its failure to grasp the importance of metapolitics and cultural efforts. As a result it has simply capitulated to the Left on these issues. Secure in the knowledge that the New Left does not threaten the ownership of property or financial power relations, the only issues European liberals and 'conservatives' alike seem to care about, the 'Right wingers' of Europe seem to be satisfied. Otherwise they have come to stand behind ideas such as equality, feminism, mass immigration, post-colonialism, anti-racism, and LGBT interests.

A 'Right' that has become part of the Left has no value, and it is time that these pathetic advocates of fatal half-measures make way for a genuine Right.

The New Right is Born

This book outlines an example of perhaps the most important attempt in the post-war period to (re)create a genuine Right. From the ruins of the old Right, an impressive array of intellectuals has emerged on the continent. The circle centred upon the French think-tank *Groupement de Recherche et d'Études pour la Civilisation Européenne* (GRECE) have had to strike a difficult balance. For those who have grown up in post-war Europe, it is easy to see politics as nothing more than a choice between Leftist utopianism, market-based liberalism, or 'neo-Nazism' and 'fascism'. This trichotomy is obviously false, but the established institutions of the Western world, being led by the Left, have long had an interest in maintaining it.

All those who wish Europe well, be it individuals, think-tanks, or parties, must operate within the parameters of this silly paradigm and find ways to strike a balance between the constant attacks from the paid preachers of hate on the one side, and their duty to their own ideas, based as they are in the history and traditions of Europe. GRECE is perhaps the one milieu that has grappled the most with this problem continuously over the past 50 years, with varying degrees of success.

Clearly, this is the problem that must be dealt with by those social movements which are trying to put an end to, or at least alleviate, Europe's distress. All 'Right-wing populist' parties are forced to respond to a political and ideological hegemony that is most often openly hostile to Europe's native populations, and thus even more hostile to whoever casts himself as a spokesman for their interests. In some cases, the adaptations such people make are minimal — as in, for example, completely distancing themselves from thugs, terrorists, and idiots, which is a prerequisite for any possibility of winning, and for their victory to be at all desirable. The friction that is growing between the various ethnic groups in Europe is a direct consequence of radical multiculturalism (both immigration itself as well as the pathological nature of those political ideologies which bear the same name), but that does not mean that the spontaneous hostility of the majority against various other groups is something which can or should be directly translated into a meaningful political project. Pressure from the 'establishment' may thus actually be a positive thing, since it forces the Right to discipline itself and create a more positive ideology and political image.

But in the meantime, those who are attempting to walk while keeping one foot on the path of political correctness and the other outside of it can also waddle off in the wrong direction, and radically so. Parties whose function it is to preserve, or rather restore, traditional European values should not be concerned with ingratiating themselves with the sworn enemies of these very same values. Refraining from vulgar expressions of 'racism' may be a demonstration of political and personal maturity, but to be 'anti-racist' is something quite different — it is to be part of a movement which is directly linked to a reckless hatred for Europe and her history.

Manic hatred of Jews, homosexuals, Muslims, or other minorities is clearly irrational, and it cannot lead to a positive political project. Nevertheless, what Europe needs today is a Right which looks toward *her own* interests, not toward those who would turn her into a tool of groups which are, at best, indifferent to her future.

The Swedish New Right Takes the Lead

At the beginning of the new millennium, the establishment's hegemony is coming apart, as the Left's ideological and wholly unrealistic interpretation of the world is more clearly betraying its weaknesses. As a result, it is being increasingly challenged by a rapidly growing number of European men and women.

This development is ongoing across Europe, even in notoriously ultra-liberal Sweden. Although Swedes have lagged behind in this regard as a result of the Left's disproportionately strong grip on our opinion-forming institutions, we are beginning to catch up. New political players have appeared and given renewed courage to those disheartened social critics who, after years of ruthless persecution, are now able to voice their opinions in the fresh air of a new political dawn. Overall, this has created optimal conditions for a broader impact of our ideas — something that is mainly visible in Sweden with the rise of the Sweden Democrats, accompanied by a rapid growth of favourable public opinion towards them.

Although the general public only sees, for the most part, the superficial aspects of this emerging paradigm shift in terms of parliamentary successes, this trend actually began much earlier. Behind the scenes of everyday politics — where we were placed against our will, since those who control the channels of mass communication were effectively blocking our writers and thinkers from participating in the public debate — activities to prepare the groundwork have now been going on for over a decade, representing vigorous efforts to promote the development and dissemination of Europe's authentic values and cultures.

If one were to give a definite starting date to these activities, one could say that the Swedish New Right was born precisely ten years ago. In 2005, a small group of Right-leaning university students in Gothenburg began to coalesce, consisting of those of us who became enthusiastically engaged by reading a number of ground-breaking works, including the original English-language edition of Michael O'Meara's *New Culture, New Right,* as well as essays by Alain de Benoist, Guillaume Faye, Dominique Venner, Pierre Krebs, and other thinkers from the continental New Right. These texts opened our eyes to this new intellectual arsenal of the Right and its explosive ideas, not least of which was the unique concept of a 'metapolitics of the Right'. Duly inspired, we launched the think-tank *Motpol* on 10 July 2006, which will celebrate its tenth anniversary shortly after the publication of this book.

For ten years, *Motpol* has conducted public outreach efforts and carried on its work, which was directed at those who wished to create something to replace the old, impotent Right, and we have gradually begun to make this a reality. *Motpol* was initially met with scepticism and hostility, not only from the Left and the liberal Right, but also from some nationalists and some of those of the 'radical Right'.

Over the years, however, we came to win greater respect from both nationalists and even the hostile Leftists, and our operations have evolved from a small think-tank with an associated blog portal into a larger network organising lectures and seminars all over Sweden. The most famous of these events is perhaps the annual conference series *Identitarian Ideas,* which has presented lectures from many of the most formidable conservative and Right-wing thinkers from across the world. Eventually, *Motpol* also became the fully-fledged online cultural magazine it is today, attracting guest columnists from across a wide spectrum of backgrounds and viewpoints.

Motpol has served not only as a think-tank and advocacy magazine, but also as a training ground for the cultivation of the new voices of the Swedish alternative Right. Many talented writers and commentators have begun their careers with us. Some have remained, others have moved on to other projects. Most have left a significant mark upon political developments in Sweden — not least in the intellectual debate — and they will certainly continue to do so for many years to come.

Parallel to *Motpol's* emergence and growing influence, we have witnessed the gradual rise of a genuinely professional alternative media network in Sweden, which today, in 2015, has begun to challenge the establishment's media. This includes a number of different publications and outlets, from the libertarian conservative flagship *Fria Tider,* which is unique worldwide for the broad news coverage it offers Swedes while operating entirely outside mainstream news channels, to *Avpixlat,* which focuses almost entirely on criticism of Sweden's immigration policies. What we can now see is a broad and powerful media network on the alternative Right that is seriously challenging the dominance of the liberal-Left media in Sweden.

Motpol also gave rise to several side projects that have had an international impact, the most prominent being the publishing company Arktos, which as of today has published over 100 titles and is the world leader among traditionalist and Rightist publishing houses. Although Arktos' staff is international, the circle around *Motpol* and the Swedish New Right has been absolutely critical to its success.

In light of Sweden's peripheral location and small population, the influence we have had on the policies and development of the European Right in recent years has been disproportionately high, and has only been exceeded by the efforts of our colleagues in France, Germany, and Hungary. This is in spite of the fact that our successes in the realm of practical politics, at least so far, continue to lag.

The systematic efforts which have been undertaken to reverse the liberal trend in Sweden and Europe as a whole are being conducted by only a small minority in our societies. But as many, including Oswald Spengler, have pointed out, it is always a dedicated minority who change the course of history. Throughout history, less organised groups have often succeeded in influencing the development of a society by applying well-developed strategies. As Mikhail Khodorkovsky, one of the Western-funded challengers to Vladimir Putin ahead of the Russian presidential election of 2016, has put it: 'A minority is influential if it is organised.'

This optimistic insight has guided the entire project of the Swedish New Right.

The Left's Impending Doom

The real Right is now making a comeback all across Europe. In region after region, country after country, we are forcing the Left's disillusioned, demoralised, and feminised minions to retreat back to the margins of society, where their quixotic ideas and destructive utopias belong. The extreme Left does not, however, take its defeat with good graces. From their quarter we are witnessing violent riots, parliamentary spectacle, and an incomprehensible fixation on the construction and support of eccentric sexual identities, as well as a renewed 'anti-fascist' struggle consisting of harassment, violence, and, in some cases, even murders of political opponents. These are all symptoms of its dwindling influence and growing desperation. For those who have studied the collapse of the Right in the post-war period, it is easy to recognise these patterns, as there is nothing new in their 'tactics'. However, our political project is of course not primarily aimed at the crazy Left. Our real task will be to comprehend and develop an alternative to liberal modernity in its entirety. This work is made easier, however, by the Left's pubescent and suicidal antics.

The Italian philosopher Julius Evola spoke of 'men among the ruins' to describe the exclusion that traditionalists and those of the true Right were relegated to in post-war Europe. Thus deprived of power, they were forced to bide their time while the world around them degenerated into the worst of modernity's excesses and decadence. They found themselves in a Europe where previously marginalised ideas from the Left—now supported by international capital—were suddenly turned into societal norms. A Europe where an anachronistic 'anti-fascism' and a hyper-individualistic, liberal version of Marxism were established as the new religions. A Europe that gave free reign to a permanent revolution against tradition, hierarchy, and the structures and values which allowed European civilisation to flourish in the first place. A Europe in which utopian nonsense gave rise to ever more bizarre and harmful social experiments. A Europe that, despite these difficult conditions and bleak circumstances, yet retains the power to turn things around, overcome the fears that afflict her, and regain control of her destiny.

We traditionalists and Rightists, who are the defenders of Europe, have now remained outsiders for over half a century. In Europe's gloomy dusk, we now step up to the front and centre. We are the forefront of the future of Europe, and we represent the eternal ideas and values that are now returning across a broad front, building something new out of the solid stones we have found amongst the ruins.

We are the men and women of the true Right. We are the defenders of Faustian civilisation. And Europe belongs to us—tomorrow and forever.

2

Metapolitics from the Right

European civilisation faces an existential crisis. Regional and national identities have long since been dissolved, and rather than having been superseded by, or merged into, a pan-European identity, they have been replaced by an egotistical, consumerist cult, which has demolished the very sociocultural and political foundations of Europe. Alien masses settle in our homelands, with the explicit support of the elites, and the peoples of our continent do nothing to protest it. To find the reasons behind, and the solution to, this crisis, we must go beyond the constructed 'truths' most take for granted; we must look behind the curtain of symbols, ethnomasochism, cultural dissolution, oikophobia, and mass media indoctrination.

Several massive challenges stand before today's Europeans. Traditional social values such as honour, dignity, the will to self-sacrifice and social cohesion, humility before the sacrifices made by previous generations, and the view of one's own generation as a link in a chain from the ancient past to the far-flung future, have been undermined for a long time. The youth of today have lost every ounce of historical memory and identity, thus losing their faith in the future as well as any overarching perspective. Because of this, they live in the here-and-now, in a constant pursuit of immediate sensual gratification. Older Europeans, by contrast, often harbour diffuse and outdated views of the society in which they live. The chain of history has been broken, and the 'now' is no longer a natural continuation of the 'then'.

Technology and science still advance. But given increasing cultural dissolution, intellectual laziness, and demographic decline, the possibilities for scientific progress in the long term will decrease. During the 2000s we have seen an increasing part of the labour force lacking adequate education and ability — a development which leaves clear marks on the labour market and the economy.

Our culture has gradually decayed, moving towards a materialist, hedonist consumer culture — the result of a slow extermination of Europe's primal culture. One of the earliest root causes of this was the toppling of the European aristocracy in the French and American revolutions. Later, it was the development of an industrialised, urbanised, and increasingly uprooted Europe. Since the end of the Second World War, an Americanised consumer and entertainment culture has been absolutely central to this process of dissolution, displacing the authentic and distinct cultures of Europe.

We live in a fragmented and relativised reality in which virtually all cultural experiences, norms, and myths have been replaced by allegedly universal abstractions lurking within terms like 'humanism', 'liberal democracy', 'tolerance', and 'human rights'.

The historical processes that began with the Renaissance and the emergence of a bourgeois materialist civilisation, culminating in the liberal revolutions of America and France, and the gradual displacement of the monarchy and aristocracy in England through democratic and liberal reforms, increased with the growth of capitalism and industrialisation, and led to the dramatic example of the Communist Revolution in Russia. Ultimately, Europe was forced into two World Wars that left her culturally and physically decimated and maimed.

The final step in this process is the influx of masses of immigrants from other civilisations who, with the tacit and unthinking consent of the ever-more rootless and culturally impoverished Europeans, have settled within the borders of Europe. These ethnic groups — given their numbers, we must speak of groups of immigrants rather than individuals — then grow and expand, to the detriment of our own peoples. Europeans do not react, politically or culturally, but let it all happen passively and in silence. The few political reactions that do occur usually address nothing but the symptoms — immigration, cultural displacement and alienation, and heightened crime levels — and shy away from its root causes.

Practicing Metapolitics

Metapolitics is a war of social transformation, at the level of worldview, thought, and culture. Any parliamentary struggle must be preceded, legitimised, and supported by a metapolitical struggle. Metapolitics, at its best, reduces parliamentarism to a question of mere formalities.

To approach the fundamental set of challenges facing Europe, it is not enough to look backwards, or react only to the latest outward signs of the deeply rooted causes behind the extinction of European culture and its peoples. We must identify the context and causes of the situation in which we find ourselves, analyse these, and then act — politically and culturally — in accordance with the conclusions we reach. What we need is thus *metapolitical* thought and action. The metapolitical analysis does not simply relate to the obvious, surface actions of everyday politics, but examines what controls and affects the development of society as a whole over the course of long periods, which relates to the underlying assumptions and consciousness of the average citizens. Metapolitics considers culture, economy, history, and both foreign and domestic policy — not simply state, party, or nation. We must understand society as a whole, as an organism, to be able to reform it in a constructive and lasting fashion.

In recent decades, most organisations working to benefit the peoples of Europe have generally chosen to utilise strategies which have been historically successful, but which are no longer relevant in a modern context. Mere imitation of past political and revolutionary victories is doomed to failure. There has and only ever will be one Caesar and one Napoleon, to put things simply. We must learn from history not only how to attain power and influence, but to understand what power in fact is, where it is actually situated, and how it is shaped.

Metapolitics is the prerequisite of politics — the dynamic of power, as it is manifested on the street and computer screen and up to the government and parliament; in the media and the press; in academia, cultural institutions, and civil society; as well as in art and culture. In short, in all the channels which communicate values perceived on an individual and collective level. This is the reason why metapolitical analysis must precede political action.

Let us once again turn our attention to the Marxist theoretician Antonio Gramsci, who played a significant role in the Communist movement of Italy at the time just before and during the Fascist regime. Their attempt to conquer the factories and thus take them out of the hands of the bourgeoisie in northern Italy during 1919–20 came to nought. In 1926, four years after Mussolini came to power, Gramsci was sentenced to twenty years' imprisonment for his opposition to the regime and remained in prison until his death in 1936. During his time in prison, Gramsci kept a series of notebooks which today offer many lessons in strategy of great importance, posthumously published as *The Prison Notebooks*.

In this work, Gramsci claimed that the state is not limited to its political apparatus. In fact, it works in tandem with the so-called civil apparatus. In other words, every political power structure is reinforced by a civil consensus, which is the social and psychological support given by the masses. This support expresses itself in of the assumptions which underlie their culture, worldview, and customs. In order for any political ideology to maintain its grip on power, it must support itself by establishing and disseminating these cultural assumptions among the masses.

At the end of the First World War, during a period marked by extreme crisis, Italy was shaken by violent conflict over labour, expropriations of farmland, and the collapse of many of its traditional institutions. The unrest reached its climax in September 1920, as trade unionists occupied the factories of the metal industry of northern Italy, which at the time was the most crucial sector of the economy, who then tried to resume production under the control of the workers. For a brief moment, it seemed like they would follow the example of their Russian counterparts and enact a revolutionary transition to a Soviet-style regime. But it was not to be. The strikes abated, the Leftist parties fragmented, and two years later, Mussolini's Fascist Party seized control of the state apparatus.

While in prison, Gramsci contemplated the reasons why the Left, during a period when the governing institutions were in disarray and the ruling class lacked the necessary means to exercise power, failed to follow through on this revolutionary development. He came to the conclusion that the explanation was to be found in ideology. Unlike many of his classically Marxist peers, he was of the opinion that the authority of the state rested on more than simply its police and judicial system. Gramsci, who was educated in linguistics, realised that the dominant social stratum controlled public discourse, and was therefore able to exercise authority over how language was used, which allowed it to make the social order it represented appear to be an entirely normal and natural state of affairs, and its adversaries as something strange and threatening.

Gramsci came to a similar conclusion regarding culture. As he saw it, the exercise of political power rested on consensus rather than force. As a consequence the state could govern, not because most people lived in fear of its repressive capabilities, but rather because it adopted ideas — an ideology which saturated society as a whole — which gave its actions legitimacy, and gave them the appearance of something 'natural'.

On the basis of this analysis, Gramsci understood why the Communists had failed to conquer political power in the bourgeois democracies. They did not possess the cultural means to do so. No one can topple a political apparatus without beforehand establishing control over the cultural determinants upon which the political authority fundamentally rests. One must first win the consent of the people by enshrining particular concepts in intellectual discourse, mores, habits of thought, value systems, art, and education.

In what the Italian theorist described as a positional war — a war in which ideas and perceptions were the main lines of division — victory would depend on succeeding to redefine the dominant values, establishing alternative institutions to the prevalent ones and undermining the extant values of the population with a view toward altering them. A spiritual or cultural revolution was thus seen as a necessary prerequisite for political revolution. Conquering political power is only the last step in a long process, a process which begins with metapolitics.

Metapolitics, simply put, is about affecting and shaping people's thoughts, worldviews, and the very concepts which they use to make sense of and define the world around them. Only when metapolitical efforts succeed in changing this basis, and the population comes to feel that change is a self-evident necessity, will the established political power — which now finds itself disconnected from public consent — begin to stumble, before finally toppling with a boom, or it may simply peter in a rather anticlimactic fashion, to be replaced by something else. Metapolitics can thus be seen as a war of social transformation, fought on the level of worldview, thought, and culture. The Left has long since learned to fight in this manner, and until quite recently it was virtually unopposed on the metapolitical battlefield. This is changing, however, and I hope that this text will serve to increase the growing Right's understanding of the necessity to engage in metapolitics.

The Metapolitical Vanguard of the Right

Taking these insights as a starting point, we can confidently state that a political movement which fails to engage in metapolitical and cultural struggle will be unable to effect lasting social changes. Any political struggle must be preceded, legitimised, and supported by a metapolitical struggle. Otherwise it is doomed to a quixotic tilting at windmills.

To constitute a metapolitical vanguard, and hence to become a vital part of the broader initiative to set Europe back on the right path: this is the primary mission of the European New Right. We view metapolitics as a multi-dimensional, non-dogmatic, and dynamic force with the potential to articulate the essence of the important issues which confront us today, and to develop perspectives which undermine and tear down both the politically correct haze in which we find ourselves, as well as the baseless feelings of guilt and self-hatred, evident to any thinking person, which are weighing the peoples of Europe down.

But metapolitics does not simply undermine and deconstruct; it creates, encourages, inspires, and illuminates. Taken in its totality, our metapolitics aims to set an authentic Right in motion; a force which is growing in strength through our own, alternative media channels, as well as through gaps in the censored channels of the establishment. This force, once it reaches critical mass, will live its own unstoppable life, broadening the narrow confines of public discourse in a revolutionary manner and paving the way for a European renaissance — a successive, irresistible social transformation which will restore dignity, strength, and beauty to Europe.

3

Points of Orientation

In times when the business of politics is usually conducted by the opportunistic and third-rate, the need for long-term and principled thought is more pronounced than ever before. The following brief points of orientation aim to summarise some of the principles which should guide those who stand for the future of Sweden and Europe.

Man and Society

- Human societies are formed and subsist as a result of a complex set of factors. Some of these factors are their inhabitants' cultural traditions and habits, languages, religions, biological traits, ethics and morality, consumer patterns, and their social, ethnic, and political identities.

- Human beings need an authentic identity and a historical context in order to feel as if they are in harmony with the societies in which they live. That need is not satisfactorily met by fluid, plastic consumer identities, or by utopian conceptions of what man should be, enforced from above. An authentic identity is founded on language, culture, identity, ethnicity, and social reality—not on opinions, sexual orientation, or media-induced impulses and artificial needs.

• Ethnic identity is today a natural point of departure for political organisation. The liberal concept of the individual, as well as the class analysis of socialism, have both been proved inadequate. Ethnic groups now constitute the fundamental factor in almost every context, and because of this constitute excellent points of departure for political analysis and practice alike.

Imperium Europa

• For many people their local, regional, or national affiliation remains the most important identity marker. Historical circumstance, however, has made these groupings insufficient, at least as political entities, for looking after the political interests of Europeans throughout the world. This was the case already during the Cold War, when the continent was cut in half by the Soviet Union and the United States, and it remains the case today, as Europe is a subordinate partner to the US, which is now in competition not only with Russia but also China, and perhaps eventually also with a resurgent Muslim world and India.

- For this and other reasons, a unified, independent Europe is necessary. A common foreign policy, a common military, and a common will to defend the interests of Europe globally is the only way in which the continent can protect itself and act politically in the world, without being nothing more than a vassal to one of the other great powers.

- The emergence of a multi-polar world has created hitherto unimagined possibilities for Europe to free herself from her subordination to the United States through purely diplomatic means. By balancing different superpowers against each other, Europe could seek and find her own way and attain a higher level of self-determination in political matters. If relatively small nations like Japan and Burma/Myanmar can accomplish a great deal by exploiting the increasing tension between China and the United States, Europe can do even more by only choosing to cooperate with superpowers which respect her sovereignty.

- Despite the need for political integration, local, regional, and national identities should be recognised, supported, granted rights, and further developed within the borders of Europe. The bureaucratic centralisation characteristic of the current European Union must be limited to areas where it is absolutely necessary; meaning primarily to security issues, trade, and foreign policy, but little else. Imperium Europa, or a European federation, to use a more modern expression, is desirable in a purely political sense, not as a means to create this or that 'new man' of a socialist or post-nationalist type. The regional and national identities of Europe should not be discarded, but rather strengthened within a pan-European framework.

Economy and Politics

- We advocate the primacy of politics over economics. Political power should be wielded in the open, by visible and responsible individuals who are answerable to the people they govern. The current state of affairs, in which corporations, organisations, or private individuals who have amassed vast power or wealth are permitted to freely influence or decide what happens in all areas of society is unacceptable. The genuine political representatives of the peoples of Europe must have the powers — and the will — to curb the corrupting influence of money from private actors in politics.

- Primacy does not equal regulation or planning. The capacity of free markets, free people, and free trade to create economic wealth should not be underestimated, and should not be limited for other reasons than curbing the influence of money in politics and dealing with social problems with which the market alone is unable to cope. The therapeutic welfare state has historically taken far too many liberties against individuals and groups in Europe, and it is well worth remembering that the majority of the victims of Communism were not shot, but starved to death on account of absurd economic policies. Furthermore, social services and aid which Europe provides for its people, such as healthcare and social security, should be limited to Europeans, and not extended to non-Europeans whose only interest in being in Europe is to selfishly take advantage of these resources which are freely handed out to them by utopian politicians and social crusaders.

- Economics is not the absolute fundament of society, and a dogmatic approach to its functions is never prudent. Alain de Benoist's words are ours as well: we'll gladly welcome a society with a market, but not a market society. Conversely, demands for economic equality for the people of Europe for its own sake must not be allowed to limit the positive, wealth-generating effects of market forces, in the way they have previously done and still do in some areas of the world.

- Spheres which are protected from the forces of the marketplace have value in and of themselves — religious communities, cultural and sports associations, local historical societies, and other such forms of community organisation are important elements of a healthy society, provided that they serve the interests of the European peoples and do not work against them.

The Peoples of the World and Ethnic Pluralism

- Our historical subject is Europe, and we first and foremost stand for and defend the interests of her and her peoples. This does not in any way preclude good will towards, or cooperation with, other peoples and political groups. However, every person in Sweden and Europe deserves political authorities who will stand for the Swedish and European peoples, when their safety or welfare is under threat, and who will seek to preserve and improve their welfare. A politician who is motivated by some obscure notion that his or her primary loyalty should be to some abstract 'humanity' or 'world', rather than the actual people being governed, can never be tolerated as a ruler, or even as a legitimate democratic representative. 'Humanity' or 'the world' are concepts which refer to no concrete political, cultural, historical, or anthropological reality, and when they are invoked they inevitable serve to disguise questionable loyalties or plain political idiocy.

- As for the role Europe should play outside of her own borders, that will be up to history. Generally, it can be said that her function should not be to force patterns of life and political systems upon other peoples for which they have not shown explicit interest. The fanatical group of warmongers who, while mouthing platitudes about human rights and democracy, kill millions throughout the world while simultaneously, using the same rhetoric to encourage mass migration to Europe from the Third World must be deprived of any influence on the foreign policy of the West. Opinions on the way other peoples handle their affairs should be expressed solely through diplomacy and example, not through the wars of aggression and attempts at subversion which time and again in recent decades have come back to haunt us.

- The principle that every people, insofar as it is possible, must be allowed to live as they want is not based on any notions of cultural relativism, in which all ways of doing things are viewed as being of equal value for all peoples, everywhere. It is, instead, strictly pragmatic: war and revolutions are without exception worse than the alternative, which is simply to leave the development of each society to the people who are actually living there. For this reason we should not wage wars or foment revolutions and otherwise subvert the established orders in others' lands.

- In return for this direct opposition to intervention and violence against cultures and peoples, we demand the same for ourselves. Mass immigration to Europe must cease. The Americanisation and the importation of stupid political ideas and an infantilising popular culture must be limited, and be replaced by a culture partly created from below by the various peoples of our continent, and partly by intellectual and cultural elites who are politically and spiritually loyal to Europe.

Parliament, Revolution, Reaction

- Parliamentary efforts can never be more than complements to broader cultural and political work. The results of elections are but products of how public opinion has been formed and how, what, and in what manner information has been spread between these elections. Our strength is that we speak of the actual circumstances everyone sees around them, as opposed to those anti-European political forces who continue to attempt to pull the wool over the peoples' eyes by painting rosy pictures for them which fly in the face of the facts. This can be transformed into favourable electoral results for parties of a more or less positive orientation, but these results are never more than a slight advantage in work that must always be carried out with a broader and longer view in mind.

- Political violence, whether organised or committed by individuals, cannot play any positive role in the rebirth of Europe. Our current political establishment is superior, to a degree which begs any historical parallel, to anyone who seeks to challenge it within its territory — not only militarily and when it comes to surveillance and intelligence. To advocate a literal 'revolt' or 'revolution' under current historical conditions is to relate to society as an angry child to a parent, trusting that one's tantrum will lead to a wish being granted simply on account of its very harmlessness. The best example of this is the 'revolutionary' Left: should an actual direct confrontation between the state apparatuses of the West and the ridiculous little hordes of Communists and anarchists who claim to want to overthrow them, the latter would be wiped off the face of the Earth within days and would be missed by none. The true Right should not seek to emulate their time-wasting idiocy. Revolutionary prattle can do nothing but agitate the mentally unstable into acts of violence which are both immoral and can have no practical value whatsoever. We should leave such acts to the extreme Left and the radical Islamists, where it comes naturally. We set higher standards for ourselves. Violence can only be problematic. Our method, once again, is the metapolitical method — the gradual transformation of society in a direction which will be beneficial to us and, more importantly, the population in general. Agents both within and outside the established political system can take part in this work, insofar as there is a will and thus a way. Revolutionary upheavals have wrought havoc on the European continent for over two centuries. The insanity ends now. The reaction is coming, step by step, and we will follow Julius Evola's recommendation to 'cover our enemies with scorn, rather than chains'.

- The success of our ideas is not only possible. It is certain.

4

How to Handle the Decline of the Left

After the Left had completed its long march through the institutions and secured its hold on opinion-shaping institutions such as the news media, radio, and television, it wasted no time in using this newfound power in the service of the outright persecution of its political opponents. This persecution began in earnest during the late '90s, and has increased in strength and tastelessness ever since. In the following two sections I offer practical tips concerning what you as an individual can — and should — do about it.

To the Politically Harassed

The Swedish persecution of political dissidents reached a new height at the end of 2013, when the worst form of muckrakers — mainly employed by the economically distraught (and hopefully soon-to-be bankrupt) tabloid paper Expressen — *collaborated with far Left extremists from the so-called Research Group/AntiFa Documentation and, through the use of questionable methods, managed to obtain the personal details of Swedish citizens who had posted comments which were critical of immigration policies on various Websites. Immediately following this event, a media witch-hunt without equal in the history of the modern Western press ensued. The following article was my immediate answer to this campaign of persecution, and was published on* Motpol *on the 13 December 2013, but it remains topical and relevant, not only in Sweden but throughout Western Europe and North America, and will probably remain so until we ourselves alter the situation to make it less so.*

This whole affair is, of course, unpleasant for those individuals who have been targeted by being among the 6,200 people registered and mapped in *Expressen*'s shaming campaign. Even so, it is also a clear sign of desperation among the Leftist cultural elites who have got used to holding a monopoly on shaping public opinion in this country in recent decades; elites which are now rapidly losing this monopoly, largely because of the Internet.

The 'mainstream media' is widely acknowledged to be dying and becomes less and less relevant with each passing day, while alternative media channels are gaining ground at a breakneck speed. Upwards of two million Swedes now use alternative media and Websites, many of which are often critical of immigration, as their primary sources of news. This is natural, since such media, whatever their other shortcomings, better reflects the reality that many people actually experience than the established media does.

The Sweden Democrats advance — despite the efforts of the established media to oppose them — in every single opinion poll. And the journalist clique, which is accustomed to being able to manipulate public opinion at will, seems unable to do anything about it. It comes as no surprise then, that they are frustrated beyond reason and stoop to desperate means such as these. These conceited moral policemen, usually all aglow with talk of compassion and tolerance, suddenly reveal their true faces and an absolute intolerance of anyone holding views they dislike, as well as a complete dehumanisation of those they deem to be their political enemies. To these humanitarians, ruining someone's life to punish him or her for something written in anger on the Internet is perfectly in order.

But do not despair. The desperation and frustration we are now witnessing among the journalist caste is a stark indication of the fact that the situation in this country is in the process of normalising itself, and could be seen as an early manifestation of the death throes of the Leftist hegemony in Sweden. It is said that it is always darkest before dawn, and dawn may come sooner than you think.

What is most urgent at this moment in time however, is to minimise any personal damage to those of you who have been afflicted, or are liable to be afflicted, by these direct persecutions. Let me give you ten simple suggestions for what can be done.

1. **'No comment'.** The journalists who contact you, or in certain cases even have the audacity to visit your home uninvited, are not worth being treated as serious professionals. They are in fact not even political opponents, but opponents of the entire Swedish tradition of free speech. Do not grace these nasty little sadists with any comments they can quote in their substandard articles. Refuse to play along. You are under no obligation to make any statements whatsoever. If you yourself ran around with a camera, asking rude questions, you would most likely be arrested for harassment. The journalists are not better people than you, and hold no special rights to harass people.

2. **Give them the welcome they deserve.** If they visit you at your home — especially if you own your own home — they are trespassing on your property. There are many creative, legal, and non-violent ways to make them vacate the premises. If you believe yourself at risk of receiving a visit from Leftist journalists, you may find it advantageous to keep a bucket of water right inside your door. This bucket may then simply be emptied right over the head of the thin, gender conscious and LGBT-certified journalist that rings your doorbell with his or her camera team. The water needn't necessarily be clean tap water. A more environmentally sound choice would be water

recycled from the last time you did the dishes, or something equivalent. As a friend of Europe, it is important to mind environmental issues.

3. **Deny everything.** In the event that you have a sensitive professional position, and are in danger of losing this position, simply deny their allegations and make sure they understand that you will sue if they publish their claims. Say nothing else. You are under no obligation to prove yourself 'innocent' simply for having made use of your right of free speech, and they have no actual evidence to present. Any information procured through hacking has no value as evidence, and could theoretically just as well have been fabricated.

4. **Litigate, litigate, litigate.** Take everything they write straight to court. Report them to relevant bodies responsible for press ethics, sue them for libel, and get yourself a lawyer. Swedish Leftist media is used to getting away with murder without any legal consequences. When engaging in this type of writing, they tend to be sloppy and irresponsible, and because of this they often violate legal limits of various sorts. This in turn makes for easily-won cases, with the possible boon of juicy damage payments. Make sure to demand especially large damages if what they published cost you your job, or made you suffer any other form of personal injury.

5. **Boycott.** Encourage all your friends and acquaintances to boycott the papers which take part in, or accept, this. There are

close to two million potential Sweden Democrat voters in this country, and a far greater number of people who are critical of immigration, or simply fed up with the mainstream Swedish media. If a significant portion of this segment of the population were to simply cease buying the smut published by the papers that participate in these Stalinesque campaigns against private individuals, their already dire economic straits may degenerate even further.

6. **Give them a taste of their own medicine.** If you are part of an activist political organisation, this offers a golden opportunity to do something good, while winning legitimacy and goodwill in the eyes of the public. The public support for what these newspapers are currently engaging in is virtually non-existent, and it may be prudent to make them answer for their actions by calling them up (record the conversation) or by visiting *them* at home with your own 'camera crew' to ask them to explain their hostile actions against freedom of speech.

7. **Stigmatise, stigmatise, stigmatise.** For years the primary weapon chosen by the cultural elite to punish those who questioned the insane social experiment of mass immigration was to attack and slander us in newspapers and on television. As we are now approaching a new situation, where newspapers make ever-larger budget cuts and unemployment among journalists is reaching record levels, the journalist clique has

fallen on hard times. Make sure to remember the names of any journalist even remotely connected to this debacle. In a not-too-distant future they may well come calling to beg for employment at a firm owned by you or an acquaintance, and their application may well end up on the bottom of the pile. Let the well-deserved increasing unemployment among the anti-free speech journalist class keep increasing, and let it reach and remain at a record high. Instead of painting ourselves as victims, which is what they want, since it has a demoralising effect and spreads the fear they want to instil in any critic of the present order — make sure you become a winner, and let the far Left paint themselves as victims.

8. **Build networks.** You should — and must — be aware that you have friends and allies at all levels of society. If you are one of the few unfortunate enough to lose your job because of this sort of nonsense, contact us at *RightOn.net*. We have a significant network, and we will do our best to help you. Likewise, if you are an employer and willing to help out, contact us.

9. **Go public.** If your life situation allows it, do the exact opposite of what our opponents want to accomplish with this campaign, and start writing under your own name. Firstly, this will contribute to the dismantling of the already-crumbling stigma surrounding our ideas, and secondly, it robs malicious opponents of the possibility to 'unmask' you. As a

side benefit, knowing that you have to defend what you write in public will decrease the risk of expressing yourself in a stupid or vulgar manner — if you want to blow off steam, you should do it in private.

10. **Last but not least: do not give up hope.** It is easy to become shocked and overwhelmed when one is targeted by an unexpected, disproportionate media campaign such as this one, simply for having made use of one's constitutionally protected right to express your opinion in a comment made online. You should remember that this is temporary phenomenon, that the whole affair will soon be forgotten, and that no one apart from the ever more cult-like Left of Södermalm, the Upper West Side, or Hampstead will be horrified by what you have written. Under no circumstances must you let these malicious, sadistic has-beens silence you. Keep criticising the politics of insanity — if possible, twice as much as before.

Do not let them win.

Dealing with Expo, the SPLC, Searchlight, and Other Hate Groups

The article which follows was originally published on Motpol *on 23 March 2015, after the far Left foundation* Expo *had involved itself in a number of events.* Expo *is essentially the Swedish version of the Southern Poverty Law Center (SPLC) of the United States*

or the scurrilous Searchlight organisation based in Great Britain,
and during its formation it had links to and collaborated with the
latter in particular. Therefore the points that this article makes are
equally relevant when dealing with any of them, or indeed any
such extreme Leftist hate groups.

Of the recent incidents involving the *Expo* foundation, the one
which received the most attention was the report that their col-
laborators from the so-called Research Group were uncovered
as the violence-mongering extremists they are, in a unique piece
of investigative journalism published in *Dagens Samhälle*. The
publisher of *Expo*, Robert Aschberg, has spent years on the same
board of at least one of the exposed 'activists', and also played a
part when they established their massive database. The connection runs deeper than this, of course, but in the hope of avoiding
and deflecting uncomfortable questions about these issues, *Expo*
has instead instigated a number of unprofessional campaigns
and attacks.

By far the most attention-grabbing one was to publish a private Facebook message from the (then) Acting Chairman of the
Sweden Democrats, Mattias Karlsson, where he asks the foundation for help in identifying the 'circle of people around *Motpol*'.
Much has already been said about this, but one can only hope
that Karlsson is truthful when he now claims to understand the
real purpose of *Expo*. If any doubt remains, I can explain to him
that the purpose of *Expo* is merely to smear and dehumanise

people who oppose mass immigration, and absolutely not to discourage extremism and violence as they claim. At any rate, the goal of helping the Chairman of the Sweden Democrats does not rank high on *Expo*'s list of priorities.

Another group which had failed to understand the nature of *Expo* was the one which recently founded the *Bildningsförbundet Forntid och Framtid* (roughly translated as the Educational Association of Prehistory and the Future). What they did not understand was the fact that people who appear in *Expo*'s massive register of personal data on political opponents are not allowed to organise under any circumstances whatsoever, even if the purpose of such an organisation is not explicitly political. They were immediately pilloried on *Expo*'s homepage with an article detailing the founding members' supposed connections to the Sweden Democrats and *Motpol*, among others. The association was promptly disbanded, and thus confirmed *Expo*'s right to decide which people are entitled to get together to discuss history, and which are not.

To avoid these situations, individuals targeted by *Expo* or contacted by them for whatever other reason, should apply the following simple principles. I can promise you that if you do, you will thank me afterwards.

1.   **'No comment'.** If *Expo* contacts you, it is preferable not to comment on anything whatsoever. You have absolutely nothing to gain by doing so. It is far better to offer a sarcastic

remark, and then hang up. Furthermore, it is a sound principle never to deal with amateur journalists from the far Left or to legitimise their unprofessional activities by answering any questions. For an alternative approach, if you feel that you have sufficient verbal know-how and fighting spirit, see point 4.

2. **Do not let them fool you.** Even if you yourself are not their present target, but are rather contacted as a source, don't let their friendly, oily tone of voice fool you. Even if the person they are researching is someone you dislike, nothing can ever justify collaborating with *Expo* to 'get back' at others on the Right, or in fact anyone at all. Furthermore, such behaviour can come back to haunt you, since *Expo* will not hesitate for an instant to publish your correspondence whenever it suits their purposes, which will severely hurt your credibility. It suffices to consider the example cited above, where the polite attempt on the part of a top Sweden Democrat to get information on *Motpol* was published on *Expo*'s site, complete with brown-nosing Christmas greeting and all. *Expo*'s employees are paid to destroy your operation, and they would very much like to destroy you personally as well. Remember that.

3. **Act like a man.** Being called a 'racist' or 'Right-wing extremist' by semi-criminal extreme Leftists is not the worst that could happen. The panicked statements by the Chairman of the previously mentioned Educational Association in which

he called certain other serious and honorable dissident groups 'madmen' for no particular reason made his pillorying far more embarrassing and painful than it needed to be. Don't bother to deny anything. Briefly inform them that you will sue them for libel. Then contact us on *Motpol*, and we will help you get in touch with a competent lawyer to litigate on your behalf.

4. **Go on the offensive.** Make sure you have an application on your phone that allows you to record conversations, and activate it as soon as it becomes clear that it is *Expo* calling. Question their activities. Ask them about their current collaboration with AntiFa and the Research Group. Ask them about their founder, who beats up his girlfriends and is a pyromaniac. Keep them on the phone by implying that you will answer their questions only as long as they answer your questions first. Then upload the call to YouTube. Merry times will be had by all.

5. **Be aware of *Expo*'s ever diminishing relevance.** We have recently lived through the most insane decades in the history of Sweden. It has been a period marked by destructive social experiments and the disproportionate influence of Left-wing extremism on media and culture. The temporary status of *Expo* as 'objective experts on Right Wing extremism' is but one of many symptoms. This tragicomic epoch is fortunately moving towards its conclusion, and *Expo*'s

increasing difficulty in recruiting competent, or even fully literate staff is a clear indication of this. Don't bother yourself with what *Expo* writes about you — in ten years *Expo* and their amateurish, libellous journalism will be nothing more than an embarrassing historical footnote.

In short: do whatever you can to hinder *Expo*'s registration and persecution of the 'politically incorrect'. Their mental terrorism works only so long as we choose to participate in their games, and accept our subordinate status as 'thought criminals' who have something to be ashamed of.

It is time to stop doing just that, and show them who should really be ashamed.

5

Brief Advice on Gender Roles

Men and women of the modern West are certainly nothing to be proud of. Sweden and Swedes are, unfortunately, no exception to this general principle. During the twentieth century we — who have historically been distinguished for being fearless and morally exemplary, or at the very least for being people of great achievements, have been declining at an increasing rate into a miserable condition. The average Swede has become cowardly, narcissistic, and timidly conformist — and has lost the ancient concepts of honour and dignity that used to occupy a prominent place in our public life. This is equally true of men and women alike, even if the degeneration expresses itself in different ways depending on one's gender.

Before proceeding, I should stress that there are obviously exceptions. I also have great sympathy for the fact that it is exceptionally difficult to live honourably in this modern, liberal society, under a culture which does everything possible to hinder and oppose every form of traditional honour, morality, and decency. Like much that is written on the radical Right, this is about principles of practical action, and there is no reason to feel offended if you have at some point chosen to do things differently.

If you are reading this book, it is fairly likely that you, in some sense, are an exception — or at least a person who intends to improve yourself. You are one of those who constitute, or will constitute, that vanguard of those frontline figures who will lead the way in the march to normalise European society and restore a traditional order. Based on this assumption, I have a number of practical suggestions to offer.

Since I, like you, saw through the Leftist myth of the absolute equality and sameness of the sexes a long time ago, this advice will be slightly different for men and women. This is for the simple reason that we are different, and these differences are fundamental, deeply rooted, and comprehensive, rather than superficial, as the Left and the liberals have been trying to make us believe for so long.

Contemporary culture does its best to undermine traditional ideals, and encourages exactly the type of repulsive patterns of behaviour which have crushed our people down to the shameful, undignified level at which they find themselves today. And, unless you had traditionally minded parents with great foresight, there is a good chance that you have never learned certain fundamental facts, which come naturally to most other peoples, something that will give you a competitive disadvantage in the ever-hardening climate of multicultural society, where the competition between different ethnic groups has thus far been marked by continual defeats and retreats by the Swedish and European side.

For Men

Sweden and Europe today face a number of serious problems. Finding solutions to these problems demands real men. Unfortunately, one of our greatest problems at this time is precisely the lack of them. The deconstruction of the European male has been an important element in — and in fact a prerequisite for — the Left's project of destruction. Their methods have been too numerous to summarise in a short chapter of a brief book, but among the most important steps which they have taken would be the reduction of the military's role in society (in the case of Sweden, the abolishing of the general draft, which thus depriving young Swedish men of an essential rite of passage), 'affirmative' action to drag women into every occupation that it is possible or impossible for them to fill, and the elimination of strong, traditional male role models from modern popular culture. The very latest innovation is the ridiculous pseudoscience of 'gender studies', the sole and express purpose of which is to deconstruct gender roles. It all amounts to a sheer attack against all forms of traditional gender roles which, under the cover of 'justice' and 'equality', aims to create an atrophied human being who is dependent on neutered academics for his or her value system.

The result of all this is confused gender identities; a society where young men achieve less and less in education, suffer from completely irrational insecurities, and even have reduced testosterone levels — far lower than have been normal since they began to be measured.

Sweden and Europe are enveloped in twilight — an utterly grave situation that demands real men for its solution, men who are willing to accept their traditional roles as defenders of family, folk, and civilisation. It is your responsibility to become such a man.

What follows is concrete advice on how to take the first steps to transform yourself into the kind of man Europe needs and deserves:

1. **Assess your physical state and your capacity for self-defence.** Unless you already do, make sure to start training physically — and I am not referring to golf, badminton, or African dance, but actual weightlifting. Furthermore, take up some form of martial arts, preferably MMA, kickboxing, or whatever else that suits your interests, provided that it includes proper sparring. In this way you get used to the idea of defending yourself against and inflicting violence. If

you ever find yourself in a situation where you are forced to use these skills, which you very well might if you live in the decaying civilisation once known as the West, this may very well prove to be the difference between life and death for you, your friends and family, and perhaps even your community itself. It is your responsibility as a man to keep yourself in shape and to be capable of defending your family and community.

2. **Free yourself from the false worldview of the Left.** Do not even consider it as anything other than a product of insane people who want to hurt you. And do not, under any circumstances, refer to yourself as a 'men's rights activist'. Doing so signals weakness, and also lacks any logical basis. Any such 'rights' are myths, and rank alongside the rest of the Leftist ideological debris. Once again: if you do not have a special proclivity for deconstructing nonsense, or some perverse interest in dumb political ideologies, do not even waste your time thinking about the ideas of the Left.

3. **Learn basic gentlemanly virtues.** This is especially important for those of us who live in the decadent postmodern West, for two reasons: firstly, because these virtues are worth preserving and passing on to coming generations; and secondly, because internalising these virtues will give you a massive competitive advantage over other modern men — spoiled and feminised as they are.

4. **Develop a healthy attitude to women in our segment of the
    political sphere.** Realise that, in general, they do constitute
    the 'weaker sex', that they are in need of protection, and that
    they do not have the same responsibility which you do in
    the struggle that lies before Europe. European, and especially
    Swedish, men, conservative nationalists being no exception,
    are unfortunately products of our corrupted modern culture
    and the Leftist indoctrination which we were subjected to
    during our upbringing. As a consequence we often make
    the mistake of viewing women as absolute equals, with the
    same responsibilities and abilities as men. From this point of
    departure, many are shocked when faced with the low per-
    centage of women who are active in our circles, and believe
    this to be a problem which could be solved if only we were
    to 'adapt our message', 'convey a softer image', or something
    similar, whereupon women would flock to us and eventu-
    ally come to constitute half of our ranks. These are of course
    erroneous conclusions, founded on completely maniacal
    premises, and the sooner you dispense with this delusion, the
    better. Women have as a rule always been underrepresented
    in political matters, with feminism as the sole exception. This
    exception not only proves the rule, but also demonstrates
    that the rule is probably both natural and desirable. Given
    the character of the political sphere, especially of its Right-
    wing elements, it is an inescapable fact that women are and
    always will be underrepresented. Because of this, the few

women who not only attach themselves to our cause, but also prove themselves competent, sometimes become the objects of exaggerated degrees of appreciation and attention, and are put on a pedestal. This is a mistake to be avoided, since it is undignified as well as impractical, and benefits neither the men nor the women involved.

5. **Relationships.** Since the so-called 'manosphere' is already bristling with articles on this subject, I will be brief and offer only three pieces of advice, which will make your life far better and simple, should you chose to apply them.

5.1. **Never make finding a woman your primary goal,** consuming all your time and attention. Access to worthy female companionship is rather a bonus and secondary effect of having succeeded in other areas of life. In short: focus on becoming a better man in terms of how your education, career, and other efforts can best serve Europe, and women will appear in your life of their own volition. When you find the right woman, make sure to start a family, preferably as early in life as possible. When you eventually find yourself on your deathbed, your sons and daughters will carry your heritage within them. The more carriers Europe has, the better.

5.2. **Think of your male circle of friends as a *Männerbund*,** where certain principles of honour pertain. One important such principle is to avoid competition over the same women, and not least staying away from friends' daughters and former girlfriends. Such issues are constant sources of conflict in male circles, and in the long run it is never worth it.

5.3. **Do not fall for the myth of equality.** This cannot be stressed enough. Men and women are fundamentally different and have different roles to play, in society as well as in a relationship. As a man it falls on you to lead the family. Never give up an inch of this leadership role — it is undignified, counterproductive, and will have catastrophic effects on both your lives, not least on your intimate relations.

For Women

If you are a woman reading this, you are truly part of a small, exclusive group, and I want to express my deepest appreciation for your interest and dedication. You also belong to that half of the population which has been most thoroughly subjected to the malicious and fanciful Cultural Marxist propaganda. It has, amongst other things, convinced you that the male role is the norm for everyone, and that it is something you should aspire to. It has put the idea into your head that you should always put education and career before family, and that 'sexual liberation', in the sense of imitating the worst aspects of male sexuality and the pursuit of multiple partners, is something that strengthens you — rather than something that damages you, as massive empirical evidence suggests it does. You are also the primary targets of the propaganda which abuses and takes advantage of emotions (empathy in particular), and promotes 'multicultural-ism', 'White guilt', and 'equality', which has led to the sad fact that today, Swedish and European women more generally tend to be far more Leftist than the men in those countries. Women consti-tute an integral component in the maintaining of the politically correct order, since they assume the role of the thought police in their daily lives much more often than men do, and do their best to hinder and punish people in their surroundings who have dared to deviate from the politically correct, Cultural Marxist norm.

If you are reading this you have probably seen through the politically correct factory of lies, and perhaps you are also aware of the facts mentioned above. Nonetheless, to make your efforts for normalising Europe as effective as possible, follow this simple advice:

1. **Get your priorities straight.** In your autumn years, having a successful career behind you will be nothing compared to having a large family, with grandchildren and everything else that comes with it. This is also the best and most natural method for ensuring your retirement benefits — a few dec-ades from now, your children and grandchildren will be far more inclined to take care of you than the rapidly crumbling European welfare states will. Besides, passing your genes on is a far worthier goal in life than slaving for some multinational

corporation, which will forget all about you the second you retire. Furthermore, the plummeting birth rates of Europe must be reversed. Make sure to have at least three children, and raise them well. In this regard, the future of Europe rests squarely in your hands.

2. **Recognise the value of your personal honour.** Forget everything contemporary society and the Left tried to make you believe in relation to the 'sexual revolution'. If you are lucky, you had good parents who raised you well and taught you the fundamental truths, such as the fact that your long-term interests are not served by having sexual relations with a man the first time you meet. Rather, restraint on the part of women facilitates the process of 'falling in love', and creates better conditions for lasting, sound relationships. Even if men try to get you into bed the first time you meet, you should view this as a test, a test which you will fail miserably if you succumb. Most men will have a lot more respect for you if you refuse, and it makes absolutely no difference whatsoever what they try to tell you or themselves about the matter.

3. **Nurture your femininity.** Realise that your feminine qualities are your greatest assets. Nurture and develop them. They are also your main weapon in the rather brutal competition which constitutes natural selection, and it is your primary strength in your interactions with men. Do not be fooled into believing that adopting male behavioural patterns are to

your advantage. The sooner in life you realise this, the more successful and happy you will be. Developing intellectually and acquiring skills are things you can always do, but imitating male patterns of behaviour and competing with men is hard enough for men. You have nothing to gain by doing so.

In Conclusion

Always strive to improve yourself within the framework of your naturally given gender role, and thus your natural role in society and the community. You may live in a depraved, undignified age, and a certain degree of adaptation may be necessary, but it is you and people like you who will form the vanguard in the reformation of European society, and the restoration of our ancient, traditional ideals. These ideals once built the great civilisation of Europe, and they will rebuild it when this age of darkness ends.

6

Metapolitical Dictionary

0–9

1914, the Ideas of

The expression 'the ideas of 1914' refers to the German reaction to the ideas of 1789: freedom, equality, and brotherhood. The expression was coined by the author Johann Plenge in his book, *Der Krieg und die Deutsche Volkswirtschaft*.[3] In a later lecture, he explicitly put the ideas which he saw Germany as fighting for in the First World War in opposition to the revolutionary ideals of 1789. In Sweden the expression was quickly adopted by the political scientist and the founder of the geopolitical school of thought, Rudolf Kjellén, who claimed that the ideas of 1914,

---

3 *Der Krieg und die Volkswirtschaft: Zwischen Zukunft und Vergangenheit nach 16 Monaten Wirtschaftskrieg* (Münster: Borgmeyer, 1915).

in contrast with those of 1789, were order, justice, and national solidarity.

A

Americanism

Americanism (also Americanisation) describes the United States' establishing of its cultural, economic, and political interests in other nations and cultural spheres at the expense of the interests and traditions which are natural to those places. The fact that the United States became recognised almost universally as the cultural centre of the world after the Second World War has made American culture self-proliferating. But cultural, as well as political and economic, Americanisation also occurs through America's very conscious strengthening of its own influence, through soft or hard means, over countries and regions across the world. Hence, this term refers to the American form of global cultural imperialism.

Americanisation is most pronounced in post-war Europe, where it was not so long ago that the liberal democratic Allies and the Communist Soviet Union stood victorious and divided Europe between themselves. Once the Soviet Union collapsed, the US was quick to extend its political and cultural tendrils into Eastern Europe as well. Because of this, American influence over

European politics, economy, and culture has been far-reaching in most areas.

Anti-liberalism

Anti-liberalism is a fundamental component of the tradition of the European New Right which opposes the globalist, egalitarian, and individualist worldview characteristic of liberalism. While liberalism rejects any form of tradition as well as ethnic and cultural identity, at best reducing them to interchangeable quantities within system driven purely by economics and a bureaucracy, these same values are to the very basis of the political positions and theories of the New Right. The New Right's critique of liberalism does not primarily direct itself against the 'free market' as such, or at sound expressions of individualism, but at the specific forms of liberalism as an ideology and practice that with good reason can be viewed as harmful.

Anti-racism, differential

Differential anti-racism is the answer of the New Right, and in particular of GRECE, to what is viewed as a lack of respect for differences which are characteristic of universal anti-racism. The originator of the term is GRECE's founder and its chief thinker, Alain de Benoist. Benoist proposes a differential anti-racism that opposes racial hierarchies and respects the differences between different peoples. He rejects all attempts to assign value judgements such as 'better' or 'worse' to races.

Anti-racism, universal

Universal anti-racism is a philosophy or attitude which views all human races and ethnicities as fundamentally the same, without any difference in traits. Universal anti-racism denies the scientifically established, inherent differences which have established the ethnic pluralism of the world, and because of this aims to combat views and political models which deny this pluralism. In practice this struggle is primarily aimed at people of European descent, even while it is possible (mainly outside of Europe and the US) to note examples where one ethnic group has condemned another for its pursuit of its own ethnic self-interests, such as in the war of ethnic Arabs against the Fur, Zaghawa, and Masalit peoples in the Darfur region of the Sudan. As a general rule, universal anti-racism supports ethnic self-assertion by minorities, so long as the minority in question is not European in nature. This is justified by references to largely imaginary, reified concepts such as 'White privilege'. The term anti-racism is usually used synonymously with universal anti-racism. The term, however, also extends to differential anti-racism.

Archeofuturism

Archeofuturism is Guillaume Faye's name for a project aimed at combining archaic, traditional ways of relating to the world with ultramodern and futurist technology. Faye defines his

Archeofuturism on a philosophical basis he dubs Vitalistic Constructivism, which draws heavily on the thought of Nietzsche and certain postmodernists. Faye describes Vitalist Constructivism as being anti-egalitarian, and says that it stands for 'realism, an organic and non-mechanistic mentality, respect for life, self-discipline based on autonomous ethics, humanity (the opposite of 'humanitarianism'), and an engagement with bio-anthropological problems, including those of ethnic groups', as well as 'historical and political will to power, an aesthetic project of civilisation-building, and the Faustian spirit'.[4] Archeofuturism is thus the application of Vitalist Constructivism within social and political reality.

Faye's belief in the inevitability and necessity of realising Archeofuturism is based on what he refers to as a Convergence of Catastrophes.

Aristocracy

Aristocracy is a term derived from the Greek *aristos*, 'the best' (originally 'the most fitting'), and *kratein*, 'rule'. Hence it means 'the rule of the best'. In the history of Europe, aristocracy has usually been synonymous with the nobility and the monarchy. According to the medieval aristocratic conception of society, a certain class in society was born to a privileged existence, with the right and the duty to rule society. Its legitimacy was partly

---

4   Guillaume Faye, *Archeofuturism: European Visions of the Post-Catastrophic Age* (Arktos: London, 2010), p. 58.

derived from the Church and Christianity, and it was and is, where it still exists, typically hereditary.

As new social classes emerged, the foundations of the power of the aristocracy were undermined. The French Revolution of 1789 put an end to the position of the French aristocracy. In other parts of Europe, such as Sweden, the aristocracy was dissolved under less violent circumstances during the nineteenth century, while the Russian nobility was exterminated by the Bolsheviks in the Russian Revolution of 1917.

In practice, all social systems develop different types of elite rule, with the criteria they use for belonging to it being comparable, if often inferior, to those of the traditional aristocratic ideal.

Assimilation

Assimilation refers to an individual or ethnic group losing itself completely in another, most commonly the majority population of a particular country. Populist parties on the Right have often argued for the assimilation of immigrants as an alternative to integration or multiculturalism. Assimilation in this context means that people should give up their existing cultural or ethnic identity, and assume a new one.

In public discourse, assimilation or integration are still suggested as alternatives to multiculturalism (multiculturalism being understood as the view that separate ethnic and cultural groups can and should live together within the same territory and state without one dominating the other, and that they should all adopt a culture which is an amalgamation of the native culture of its various groups). The idea of assimilation has been rendered largely irrelevant by the developments of the early twenty-first century, since mass immigration has made cultural and ethnic assimilation impossible without the use of unreasonable and coercive measures.

B

Biopolitics

Biopolitics is a term coined by Michel Foucault. Foucault described biopolitics as the art of exercising power through regulating people's biology — power over bodies, life, and death. Biopolitics works on both a micro and a macro level, administering the living conditions of a population. According to Foucault's definition, biopolitics is a politicisation of life itself.

As a political and social phenomenon, biopolitics has a long history, and may be viewed as an accepted practice constituting a part of the modern territorial state's exercise of power. It is then a matter of controlling the physical circumstances of life of the citizens of the state, such as physical and mental health. A basic example of biopolitics is the various forms of public health projects.

Bioculture

Bioculture is the interplay of culture and biology. Man is a cultural and biological being in the sense that he, apart from his biological heritage, has developed a 'second nature' in the form of culture.

While biological conditions tend to develop slowly, and hence remain relatively constant, culture expresses itself through time in a more mutable fashion. But even culture has its constants, which collectively create and recreate a corresponding identity among the participants in the culture. This bioculture is central to the New Right's concept of identity.

The common European bioculture has a history that stretches back at least 40,000 years in time. Despite its cultural variations during this period, this bioculture constitutes the common denominator that brings the peoples of Europe together into one primary group, and makes it meaningful to speak of and seek a specific, meta-ethnic identity.

C

Catholic Social Teaching

The social teachings of Catholicism are founded on the political and social doctrines which have historically been defended by the Catholic Church. Its main point is the creation of Catholic states in which the traditional teachings of the Church are reflected in all institutions and in all relationships between people. Important issues to it are the sanctity of marriage, the prohibition of abortion and contraceptives, the right of parents over the state to raise their own children, opposition to what is viewed as false religious teachings such as Islam, and the limiting of the state in relation to civil society. Catholic social teaching is counter-revolutionary and closely connected to monarchism.

Civil society

The term civil society in its broadest application refers to all institutions and agents in a society which are not directly subordinate to the state. The civil society of a country can be seen as an important factor in determining the ability of the population to develop strong social capital.

In contemporary usage, the word usually designates those areas of society which are self-organising in such a fashion that they fall outside the purview of the market as well as the state. A few examples are the Church, trade unions, local historical societies, athletic associations, and charities.

Conservative Revolution

'Conservative Revolution' is a superficially contradictory term, mainly referring to ideas which were circulating in some intellectual circles in Germany during the era of the Weimar

Republic. These ideas formed a radical critique of the liberal programme of the French Revolution (cf. 1914, Ideas of). Nietzsche
is often mentioned as one of its important predecessors, and the
Conservative Revolution proper is thought to have included such
thinkers such as Ernst Jünger, Oswald Spengler, Carl Schmitt,
and Martin Heidegger, amongst others.

The term was coined and introduced by the poet Hugo von
Hofmannstahl and the jurist and political theorist Edgar Julius
Jung. The foremost historian of the Conservative Revolution is
Armin Mohler, who described the particulars of its ideas in his
work, *Die Konservative Revolution in Deutschland 1918–1932*.[5]

Consumer society, consumerism

Consumer society is a somewhat derogatory term, referring
to the lifestyle which is typical of the majority of the Western
world's populations today. The term came into use during the
environmental and social movements of the 1970s, and aims
to describe such phenomena as people acquiring products and
services because of artificially created appetites, rather than due
to actual needs or authentic desire. The term is used by several
disparate political movements, including anti-modernists and
environmental activists.

One effect of the consumer society is the mass production of
goods in relatively impoverished countries of the 'Third World',

---

5   *Die konservative Revolution in Deutschland 1918–1932: Grundriß ihrer
    Weltanschauungen* (Stuttgart: F Vorwerk, 1950).

usually former colonies, where regulations may be less stringently enforced and in which intensive exploitation of natural resources and human labour is possible, which are then imported back to the 'First World'. This contributes to a squandering of often limited natural and human resources, since cheap labour yields low costs of production, and hence low prices for consumers in other parts of the world.

More broadly, consumer culture as a way of life has contributed to the tendency of people to identify with the goods they purchase rather than with their ethnic or community identities. An identity built on the products one can afford to buy has emerged, and social status is increasingly defined (as opposed to emphasised or demonstrated) by one's ownership of particular items of clothing, furniture, cars, and other products.

Apart from the problematic consequences this has on an individual level, such as the incurring of debt for the purpose of acquiring disposable and unnecessary goods, the rootlessness of our age is in part a consequence of the partial and inadequate construction of artificial identities which are typical of consumer culture.

Counter-revolutionary

Thinkers and movements are defined as counter-revolutionary insofar as they oppose the revolutionary forces which have been breaking down traditional Europe for centuries, and which therefore resist the heritage of the French Revolution its ideals.

Examples of authors in this tradition are Joseph de Maistre, Plinio Correa de Oliveira, and Thomas Molnar. One of the first and most famous examples of counter-revolutionary rebellion is the Vendée uprising in France during the mid-1790s, but all across Europe frequent uprisings in defence of the traditional values and hierarchies of the continent have occurred throughout modern history. The Swedish Dacke War of 1542 may be viewed as a counter-revolutionary revolt, since among other things it defended organic institutions, as well as the traditional celebration of the Catholic Mass.

In a French context, the words legitimist and monarchist are virtually synonymous with the counter-revolutionary; examples include Charles Maurras and the organisation he founded, the *Action Française*. Other examples of movements fighting for monarchy, local and regional liberty, and Catholic or other forms of Christian traditionalism would include Carlism in Spain, the White sides in the Russian and Finnish civil wars, and the Cristeros of Mexico who fought the Masonic state which had been established there during the 1920s. Dollfuss in Austria, Franco in Spain, and Salazar of Portugal are other examples of more or less explicit counter-revolutionaries.

Convergence of Catastrophes

The Convergence of Catastrophes is the term employed by Guillaume Faye to describe a situation where modernity is confronted by a series of dire catastrophes which occur within a short period of time, which according to Faye are the consequences of the shortcomings of modernity, liberalism, and egalitarianism. Faye claims that these catastrophes lurk right around the corner, and are likely to occur in our own lifetime.

The possible catastrophes identified by Faye include ecological, economic, and social collapse; ethnic strife and civil war; and wars and terrorism on a scale which has not yet been seen. Some form of Third World War and a conflict between the aging Northern hemisphere/Septentrion and a revanchist Global South form part of his scenario.

Faye claims that this series of disasters will force a reaction among the European peoples in the shape of Archeofuturism (see above). If they do not act, they will perish.

The theory is similar to the one proposed by Immanuel Wallerstein in his book *The End of the World as We Know it.*[6]

Cosmopolitanism

Cosmopolitanism is the view that all human beings, taken together, form a total community on account of their common biological humanity. The opposite of cosmopolitanism is communitarianism, which speaks of actually existing communities and affiliations, and which denies that any overarching universalism exists which renders them all fundamentally the same. Strict cosmopolitanism views all intermediaries which distinguish

---

6   *The End of the World as we Know it* (Minneapolis: University of Minnesota Press, 1999).

individuals or groups from a posited general humanity as un-
ethical or false, and is thus hostile to nationality, ethnicity, and
religious particularism. The goal of the cosmopolitan becomes,
either explicitly or implicitly, the World State, and thus of the
concept of World Citizenship as against a national, regional,
ethnic, or religious identity.

Modern cosmopolitanism emerged from the Enlightenment,
during which it constituted an application of universal ideals
to the concept of citizenship. Cosmopolitanism today may be
defined as the founding myth of globalisation, even if it is most
likely perceived as a reality by insignificantly miniscule elites in
commerce, business, the mass media, and academia.

Cultural struggle

Cultural struggle, from our perspective, can be described as an
intellectual and creative defence of European culture. A political
struggle which is not accompanied, justified, and supported by
cultural struggle is doomed to failure.

A dynamic culture based on ethnic identity is — along with
the fundament provided by the people in itself — a condition for
the survival of the people. Political movements which neglect
cultural struggle and decline to engage in cultural activities
aimed at promoting identity will never accomplish any lasting
social change.

Cultural struggle cannot limit itself to simply defending our
heritage and our traditions or to strengthening our historical

consciousness — it must also encompass our creativity. In order to salvage European culture it is not enough to condemn its destruction — its rescue demands a well-planned, constructive, and strategic counteroffensive.

Culture

Culture is the conscious refinement of the intellectual, artistic, social, and spiritual realms. It includes religion, art, science, education, teaching, child rearing, worldview, customs, mores, and anything not strictly biological in a limited sense. Cultural questions are those which concern the spiritual tasks of society. At times, the term is contrasted with nature.

In common usage, the word tends to refer to the external attributes of a given society. These attributes are things such as art, poetry, food, dance, and other concrete phenomena which can be seen or touched. In a deeper sense, culture can be perceived as the fundamental properties of a people which have given rise to its external attributes, so that the visible culture is a reflection of the fundamental characteristics of the population. From this point of view, a people is its culture, and the culture is its people.

Cultural Marxism

Cultural Marxism is a broad term referring to the proponents of Critical Theory, and more generally to the metapolitical influence of the Left upon political and social discourse. Cultural Marxism is a meta-ideology based in a quasi-Marxist analysis of power structures and patterns of dominance. Put simply, classical Marxism posits that capitalism produces a society in which the power relations between the dominant and the working classes are unbalanced, which in turn creates a social tension which in the long run can and must be resolved by the creation of a classless social system. Conversely, Cultural Marxism discusses patterns of dominance in areas such as these:

- Gender (man/woman)
- Family (nuclear family/'alternative' family)
- Sexual orientation (heterosexuality as basis of society/LGBT)
- Race (most commonly, White/non-White)
- Culture (European/non-European, Western/non-Western)
- Religion (Christianity, rationalism/atheism, typically accompanied by an advocacy for Islam and other minority religions)

Cultural Marxism at an academic level employs Critical Theory to question norms and standards, and to alter culture to benefit supposedly oppressed groups and, not least, their self-appointed representatives (the Cultural Marxists themselves). A popular and propagandist manifestation of Cultural Marxism is so-called 'political correctness', in which powerful media channels and social scientists make it a mandatory exercise to 'question norms', and to maintain an unquestioningly favourable view of groups which are marketed as being oppressed. In consequence, the spirit of the times is changed in favour of feminism, multiculturalism, LGBT rights, atheism, and so forth. Criticising White, heterosexual, Christian White males living in nuclear families for being simultaneously hopeless bores and vile oppressors is central to the Cultural Marxist Left, and everyone under its influence.

While Communism, as Marx envisioned it, offered the resolution of class conflict in a utopian social system, all Cultural Marxism offers, even at the purely theoretical level, is a desolate form of eternal warfare between ever more narrowly defined groups of offended minorities. The only meaningful consequence that its wider application could possibly have is the ultimate extinction of European culture, which somewhat ironically would eliminate every last tendency toward tolerance of those groups supposedly which are allegedly reaping the advantages of the whole process.

In the practice of Cultural Marxism can be found an ambition to define and redefine words and terms, in order to employ them politically. By influencing the common use of language, Cultural Marxism introduces new perceptions of what it means to say or think certain things. Renaming illegal immigrants 'undocumented workers' and ethnic discrimination 'affirmative action' are two American examples of this type of distortion at work. The Swedish media channels are so ripe with neologisms that some constructions lack any corresponding terms in other languages.

The roots of the tradition of ideas we call Cultural Marxism are to be found in what is commonly called the Frankfurt School, but exactly who coined the term is not clear. Authors such as Douglas Kellner, Paul Gottfried, Christopher Lasch, Kevin MacDonald, Michael E Jones, William Lind, Tomislav Sunic, and Pat Buchanan have all used the term. Kellner, an advocate of Critical Theory himself, has defined it as a development of twentieth century Marxism, and has stated that it is an ambition of Western Marxists to apply Marxist theory to cultural phenomena and their relation to ideology and the means of production.

Kevin MacDonald, Paul Gottfried, Michael E Jones, and William Lind have likewise expanded upon a tendency among the late Western Marxists, beginning with Max Horkheimer, to bring Marxist sociology together with Freudian psychoanalysis. One example is Theodor Adorno's critique of Christian, White males in his work *The Authoritarian Personality* (1950),[7] which incorporates sociological and psychological 'observations' and analyses in order to define parenthood, pride in one's family, Christianity, adherence to traditional general roles and attitudes towards sex, and the love of one's own country as pathological phenomena.

This tendency to pathologise opinions and life patterns which are not in accordance with its own political ends is characteristic of Cultural Marxism. Differing views are often seen as irrational

---

7   *The Authoritarian Personality* (New York: Harper, 1950).

fears of the unknown — 'phobias'. Cultural Marxism claims to be tolerant of different opinions, with the notable exception of all opinions which in any significant way differs from its own. A person unwilling to live as a minority in an area dominated by Muslim Islamists may be decried as an 'Islamophobe', since it is seen as phobic and sick to want to prefer to live in one in which there is actual security for him, his family, and his children, and where he can actually live among people who are ethnically and culturally similar to himself — none of which has any value to the Cultural Marxist.

In societies with a primarily European population, the Cultural Marxist always sees the majority population as privileged and oppressive, regardless of whatever ethnic power relations and demographic proportions actually exist in the areas or spheres being analysed, regardless of whether the oppressed minorities have chosen to immigrate there or not, and regardless of whether any discernible oppression is actually taking place. Conversely, this is not seen as pertaining to South Africa, where the European minority is subject to massive judicial and institutional discrimination, quite apart from being beaten and murdered at an alarming rate. White minorities are never seen as oppressed groups by Cultural Marxists, so long as any of its members are economically or politically successful.

Cultural nationalism

Cultural nationalism (Swedish: *Kulturnationalism*) is a word which is used to distinguish Swedish nationalists who advocate for assimilation or integration of immigrant groups, from nationalists who advocate for repatriation or segregation of non-assimilable immigrant groups. In consequence of ever-increasing mass immigration in recent decades, and the corresponding impossibility of either assimilating or integrating the groups in question, the concept has lost much of its relevance.

E

Egalitarianism, anti-egalitarianism

Egalitarianism is the view that people are of equal value in all respects, and either have or should have the same possibilities, options, and resources available to them. Its most radical expression is Communism.

Anti-egalitarianism, by contrast, recognises inherent differences and their significance for shaping society. Mechanical, quantitative measurements cannot be applied to all individuals, for each one must be judged in terms of his or her personal capacity and proclivities. These differences should be used to determine the division of tasks and functions in given contexts, as well as in society as a whole.

According to anti-egalitarianism, this division is a definite good, and differences are not necessarily categorised in terms of how 'good' or 'bad' they are. Rather, they are viewed as collaborating, complementary parts, which taken together form an organic, social, and unique cultural unit which can then form the basis for a community. This line of reasoning is connected to the New Right's ideas about organic humanism and democracy, as well as the right to difference.

Ethnicity

An ethnic group is a collection of human beings who identify fundamentally with each other on the basis of common inherited, social, cultural, linguistic, and national experiences. Membership in an ethnic group is defined by sharing in common things such as cultural heritage, ancestry, founding myths, history, country, language and/or dialect, religion, appearance, genetics, mythology and ritual, food, clothing, art, and many other factors. A combination of these various components contribute to the construction of an ethnicity which represents differences between various ethnic groups.

Ethnocentrism

Ethnocentrism is a term used to describe how an ethnic group, or a person belonging to such a group, view the surrounding world from the standpoint of their own perspective and interests.

It was coined by the American social scientist William Graham Sumner (1840–1910).

Sumner's original definition of ethnocentrism was the view that the fact of one's belonging to one's own group constituted the central point from which the rest of the world is evaluated. The history, culture, norms, customs, and language of the group itself is the benchmark used when relating to other groups.

Ethnocentrism is and has always been the fundamental orientation among all peoples and cultures throughout history. Examples abound in the history of ancient Egypt, India, the Arab world, the Japanese, the Jews, the Chinese, the Mesoamerican Indians, and all other ethnic groups and cultures of which we have any knowledge.

Ethnocentrism is sometimes contrasted with cultural relativism — the view that each culture and person should be understood and judged according to its own internal context. Both perspectives have been criticised for tending towards value relativism in general, and making it difficult to defend such things as universal human rights. The New Left and postcolonial theoreticians tend to advocate ethnocentrism for 'subordinate' groups, but self-effacing universalism for others — and for Europeans in particular.

Ethnocracy

An ethnocracy is a society where most of the power in a state or territory is primarily held by a specific ethnic group, which may be the native population, or in some cases minorities who arrived through immigration. Examples of states that may be considered ethnocracies are apartheid-era South Africa, Israel, Estonia, and Latvia.

Ethnomasochism

To be an ethnomasochist is to view and approach one's own ethnic identity with shame, suspicion, and/or contempt. In its contemporary European form, ethnomasochism views ethnicity from a Manichean, dualist perspective where mankind is divided into 'White' and 'coloured' peoples, and the former is inherently morally obligated to the latter. An opposing, or even nuanced, perspective on power relations and guilt is unthinkable from the viewpoint of history and society that is held by White ethnomasochists. Ethnomasochism is constructed and expresses itself on both the collective and individual level, formally as well as informally, and as both an emotional state and in the shape of lines of reasoning founded on ideology. A similar American term is 'White guilt'.

Ethnomasochism is primarily cultivated in countries which have been influenced by ideas connected to Critical Theory, and thus with Cultural Marxism. Any shortcomings on the part of ethnic minorities are habitually blamed on European peoples. Through massive propaganda efforts — mainly in the media, but also from various ethnic and political lobby groups — European peoples are unconsciously conditioned to assume responsibility for problems supposedly emerging from caricatures of events from their history, which in reality are often the result of the contemporary failings of non-Europeans and those who champion them.

Ethnic consciousness

Ethnic consciousness is an umbrella term which can be used to describe either a political orientation in which ethnicity and belonging play an important part, or else an increase in ethnic sentiment amongst a certain group.

When several ethnic groups coming from radically different origins interact within a given geographical or political territory, the result is often social tension between them. One reason for this is the strengthening of ethnic consciousness among the majority population due to the presence of other ethnic groups, who tend to emphasise and fortify their differentiating cultural and ethnic markers in response. This dynamic can be credibly seen as one explanation of the many problems connected with multiculturalism and mass immigration. Minorities tend to close ranks and strengthen their ethnic particularities, while the majority culture reacts to the recent arrivals with hostility.

Eugenics

Eugenics is an applied science, often accompanied by a social movement, which aims to improve the hereditary characteristics of a specific group. It is usually advocated for in connection with human groups.

The term is derived from Greek *eugenes* ('well born').

Eugenics has been seen as being closely connected to racial theories. In Sweden as well as other countries, the terms 'racial hygiene' and 'racial improvement' were used interchangeably with 'eugenics' during the twentieth century. Eugenics, however, is not necessarily limited to specific ethnic groups or races, but could theoretically be applied to the human species as a whole, or to purely artificial groupings such as all inhabitants in a given area, regardless of their genetic proximity. Eugenics has also, on somewhat more shaky grounds, been associated with Social Darwinism.

Eugenic policies may vary from controlled procreation (called 'breeding' when applied to plants or animals), to 'softer' policies such as simple information campaigns or economic incitements to child rearing directed at specific groups.

Europe

Europe is the original homeland of the European peoples, and will always be the most important one, as well as being one of the seven continents of the world.

Eurosiberia

This a term coined by the French philosopher Guillaume Faye, who uses the terms Eurosiberia or Septentrion to describe the geopolitical and biocultural entity he is fighting for. Eurosiberia encompasses Europe and the Asian part of Russia, from the Atlantic to the Pacific coast. He also envisions this as a possible political entity in the future.

G

Geopolitics

Geopolitics is a scientific discipline which studies the political, sociological, and historical dimensions of the geography of the world, including how geography influences language, culture, and politics. Geographical space is not viewed by it as being shaped solely by geology, nature, or by the various populations dwelling within it, but also by political and social principles which pertain to actual and imaginary territories alike. Geopolitics is also a method for developing foreign policy which attempts to understand and explain international relations in terms of geographical and demographic considerations.

Geopolitics as a term was coined at the beginning of the twentieth century by Rudolf Kjellén, a Swedish politician and professor of political science. Kjellén in turn was inspired by theories formulated by Sir Halford J Mackinder and the German geographer, Friedrich Ratzel.

H

Hierarchy

A hierarchy is an organisation or a system in which the roles of the agents participating in it are carefully defined in terms of authority and subordination, as well as in terms of how particular duties are assigned to specific segments within it which hold the specific qualifications and resources necessary to carry them out. Unlike democratic and socialist social systems, in which the entire collective retains authority over each individual through a body of representatives, or totalitarian forms of organisation in which a dictator or single party does the same, hierarchical structures organised on a traditional basis make it possible to establish broad autonomy within each particular level, while limit political control to those sectors where it is necessary for the functioning of society as a whole.

The hierarchical principle illustrates better than anything else the foremost paradox of the dominant egalitarian paradigm. Modern ideology tends to reject every form of hierarchy and authority in theory, while keeping both very much alive in practice. The opinions of academics and pundits carry far more weight than those of others; sometimes with good reason, sometimes — as when it comes to professors of gender studies and journalists with the right sort of views — for no discernible reason whatsoever. Politicians go far beyond the mandates they have been formally granted by the will of the people, ignoring reality just as they ignore the wishes of the population they claim to represent. Forms of hierarchy as well as totalitarian tendencies live and prosper in our supposedly tolerant liberal democracy, as does hypocrisy.

History, End of

The End of History is the much-discussed thesis of the American neoconservative thinker Francis Fukuyama, in which he postulated that the end of the Cold War would also mean the end of ideological strife in the world, since liberal democracy and capitalism had allegedly proven their superiority over all other ideologies and stood victorious. Later developments, in particular the rise of political Islamism and illiberal democracies such as China, have largely proven him at least partly wrong. To many Western politicians and pundits, the global victory of liberalism is the ultimate goal, with an importance far exceeding the well-being and security of the peoples they are supposed to govern and keep informed.

I

Identity

Derived from the Latin *idem* ('the same'), identity refers to the attributes and self-identification of an individual or group of people, which is assumed to be consistent over time. Ethnic identity can be viewed as being central to well-functioning societies (see Ethnicity).

Imperium

Imperium (in Latin meaning 'command', 'authority', or 'mastery') originally signified the authority of a Roman official, an authority which was granted to him by the Senate, for a limited period of time and usually within a limited sphere of action. Later, the word became synonymous with a larger political organism which likewise exercised authority over its subjects.

An imperium can be defined as a form of social and political organisation characterised by a centre (traditionally, an emperor) which represents a religious or sacred principle. All traditional empires were founded on such a principle. Beyond this, the concept allows for a significant amount of pluralism and autonomy for the regional, religious, or professional groups which exist within it.

Imperialism

Imperialism is a theory or practice which claims the right of one people, economic structure, or ideological orientation to rule over the territories of others. Historically, imperialism was based on the various stages of development or aptitudes of different ethnic groups, so that nations which were held to be (in their own estimation) more highly developed assumed a leadership role over others, which was often established through war, cultural subversion, and/or economic exploitation. Today, the main expression of imperialism is the global expansion of modern Western liberal democracy and its ideology of human rights, as well as the economic and political interests connected to them. China's relationship with the other countries along the Pacific Ocean, as well as the country's massive expansion into Africa, has been interpreted by certain commentators as a latent form of imperialism, even if it has yet to mature.

Individualism

Individualism is the core value of liberalism and stresses the needs of the individual over those of the community. The individual is thus viewed as the sole basis of society. It would indeed be difficult to deny the central political importance of individual human beings, since particular persons are ultimately the ones who experience and are affected by political and social circumstances. As the primary or sole tool with which to interpret political realities and make political decisions, however, it is inherently problematic, since it tends to ignore obvious structural factors such as ethnicity, culture, and common interests. It is also unclear how an atomised individual can be said to possess any 'rights' by virtue of the simple fact of existing, as opposed to acquiring them in relation to the role one occupies as part of a group. As an overarching normative system, radical individualism leads to self-destruction, since ethnic and political groups which work collaboratively can always undercut and out-compete any group whose members lack solidarity within their group. Because of this, radically individualist liberalism destroys not only the group or people who apply it absolutely, but also those values it claims to defend.

Interregnum

An interregnum is a period of time connecting the end of one era to the beginning of a new one. It is a transitional period and a potential turning point in which new ideas and worldviews struggle to become hegemonic in the future.

Certain philosophers have characterised the present time as just such a transitional period, marking the end of modernity.

L

Legitimation, negative

Negative legitimation is a term employed by Guillaume Faye to describe political organisations which legitimise their own position of power, mainly by threatening the public with the potential consequences of the rise of a competing political force. The phenomenon is typical in France, where established parties have claimed that the Right-wing National Front represents a threat to democracy and peace which legitimises their own hold on power. In Sweden this tendency has, as in so many other cases, assumed ridiculous proportions. Many politicians in the Swedish *riksdag* (national parliament), as well as many in the establishment's media, spend almost as much time rambling on about the supposed dangers of the Sweden Democrats as they do speaking of actual social and political issues, or their own political views.

Liberalism

Liberalism, in the European sense in which the term is used, is an ideology which posits that a people consists of a collection of individuals who are equal in rights, and who inhabit a given territory. The state, in the liberal view, can be likened to a publicly traded company, and the citizens to its partners or owners. The state emerges through a mutual agreement between all the citizens, and because of this it is subject to their collective will as determined by elections. In this view, industry and commerce have also been created through the efforts of particular individuals, and because of this should develop through competition, and with a minimum of interference from the state. According to this doctrine, by allowing the reason of the individual to develop under the influence of politics and economics, the goal of liberalism — the greatest 'happiness' for the greatest number of citizens (utilitarianism) — is attained. Intangible social factors such as religion and tradition can be tolerated, but must be excluded from the workings of the state, lest they cause one group of citizens to attempt to force others to accept their values and traditions.

Liberalism is democratic, capitalist, and rationalist. Taken to its logical extreme, it can never be nationalist, since its conceptual framework cannot account in any substantial way for human circumstances connected to ethnicity, language, religion, or culture. Its greatest strength is in the economic field, were its application has yielded massive and impressive successes. Its main weaknesses are that its view of the state is mythical, in the sense of being false, and that its anthropology, when applied to anything outside the market, fails to correspond with what we know about the characteristics and nature of human beings.

M

Metapolitics

Metapolitics is about spreading ideas, attitudes, and values in a society, with the long-term goal of effecting a deeper political change.

The term refers to a method of influencing public opinion which does not need to be bound up within a particular party or programme. Metapolitics is an important complement to ordinary political activity, but does not replace it.

From the secret societies of the French Revolution to modern think-tanks, lobbies, and interest groups, metapolitics has always been necessary to prepare the ground for political transformations of societies, as well as to reinforce the position of established regimes.

A typical metapolitical formation of public opinion works in multiple directions: it attempts to influence both policymakers as well as the general public. It schools an activist elite ideologically, but also seeks paths to reach a wider audience with its message.

Modernity, modernism

Modernity is a term referring, among other things, to the social and political order that developed out of the Enlightenment, based on rationalist and scientific principles, as well as individual rights. The term modernism is often used to describe the art, culture, and values which are connected to this social and political development.

N

Nation, nationalism

The word nationalism stems from the French *nationalisme,* as well as from the Latin *natio/natalis,* meaning 'birth'. Related words are nativity and nature, as well as the French *Noël.* Nations are, as the origins of the word somewhat illustrates, originally expressions of ethnic and blood relationships, and all forms of nationalism are based on the different types of community and kinship within the borders of a given nation. While ethnic nationalism predates and transcends given states, modern nationalism generally celebrates a particular nation-state and its peoples, cultures, histories, and other man-made particularities.

Nation-state

A nation-state is a state populated primarily by people of one ethnicity. The nation-state, ideally, is comprised of a single ethnicity organised as a society and in possession of a state covering a specific territory.

Nihilism

Nihilism, from the Latin *nihil* ('nothing'), is a philosophical view which claims that nothing possesses an intrinsic moral value or meaning, and that objective knowledge and truth do not exist.

O

Organic humanism

Organic humanism is based on a view of human nature closely related to anti-egalitarianism. From this perspective, the living community which shapes society and its inhabitants can be likened to a living organism, in which the different parts are complementary and dependent upon one another. This organic social community fosters personality in its participants, assimilating their differing and varied abilities into an identity-affirming community and culture with a common origin and destiny.

Organic humanism can be compared to mechanical humanism, in which man is instead made into a conforming and rootless individual, and society is viewed as a machine whose parts are interchangeable and disposable. The European New Right seeks to form a counterweight to this mechanical view of society, and to employ organic humanism to defend cultural pluralism and the right to difference and identity.

P

People, will of the

The will of the people is a concept mainly discussed in democracies, but which has had a certain relevance in Communist and fascist countries as well. The term describes an ambition or a consciousness common to a people or the great majority of citizens in a nation-state.

The most common view of the nature of the will of the people in modern times is that it manifests itself through universal elections, or — as it is understood among anarchists or libertarian socialists — through collective action of various types.

Among certain conservatives who have been inspired by de Maistre, we find the notion that the will of the people can manifest itself as an instinct among the geniuses of a young people.

In late modern states such as Sweden, where the concept of democracy is becoming ever more a question of the maintaining of given dogmas and value judgements rather than for the representation of the public, references to the will of the people are now very uncommon.

Political correctness

Political correctness is a pejorative normally used for a set of values and opinions from which individuals are not allowed to deviate without falling victim to social and/or media sanctions. In particular, the term is used to describe supposedly 'sensitive' innovations in language, geared towards dominating the public discourse by manipulating people's thoughts through language.

In contemporary Europe, the term is primarily used to designate a self-righteous, Leftist attitude to politics and morals, in particular in relation to questions such as immigration, sexual deviance, multiculturalism, democracy, and gender roles. Leftist attitudes to such questions are commonly described as 'politically correct'. The term can also be applied to the methods utilised to maintain the hegemony of the politically correct orientation.

Political correctness can be more broadly understood as a loyalty to values supposedly self-evident in a given society, but must not be understood as those values which are held by the majority of the population. Rather, it is characterised by those held by individuals who share the opinions of the sociopolitical elites — the so called 'establishment'.

Populism

Populism (from the Latin *populus*, or 'people') is a political doctrine or method which aims to score political points and defend the supposed interests of the people against an elite. The populist is characterised by a will to represent an interest (that of the people), without necessarily having any particular ideological foundation. The term is today employed by the mass media to attack parties which are critical of immigration in particular, but as of late it has also been used to brand Leftist parties which question globalisation, free trade, or deregulation in some substantial way.

The origin of populism may be sought in the late Roman Republic, where two political factions, the Populares and the Optimates, fought for political supremacy in the Roman Senate. The Populares did not consist of representatives of the plebeian class, as one might have thought, but of Roman patricians who realised that one could build a political power base by courting the support of the commoners. They advocated reforms, such as strengthening the influence of the tribunes of the plebs, redistributing state land, offering a bread dole for all Roman citizens, and so on.

The most well-known leader of this faction was Gaius Julius Caesar, who would put an end to the Republic. Against the Populares stood the more conservative faction, the Optimates, whose political project was centred on preserving the Republic.

Modern populism has its roots in various American political movements.

Postmodernity

Postmodernity refers to a condition which supersedes modernity (see above). The term has many different meanings depending on the context in which it is used, but one of the most relevant interpretations focuses on the breakdown of the 'grand narrative' spoken of by the French philosopher Jean-François Lyotard in his 1979 work, *The Postmodern Condition*.[8] If the Enlightenment, the nineteenth century, and the first half of the twentieth were characterised by overarching ideologies and grand narratives, postmodern society tends to be constituted by 'small narratives'. Small groups and single individuals create their own, often disparate, 'narratives' by which they relate to the world around them. Postmodernity, then, is related to phenomena such as multiculturalism, individual narcissism, subcultural egocentrism, and the dissolution of peoples and nations amidst the breakdown of social cohesion into nonsensical quarrelling over minor issues and the grievances of self-obsessed factions.

The advocates of postmodernity are, as might be imagined, primarily to be found on the Left. At the same time, the process of dissolution also creates possibilities for the majority populations of Europe to resume those narratives which were interrupted

---

8   *The Postmodern Condition: A Report on Knowledge* (Minneapolis: University of Minnesota Press, 1984).

and suppressed during the time of those centralised states and value systems of the twentieth century which were based on rationalist and Enlightenment principles. The French think-tank GRECE has discussed how the tools of postmodernism can be understood and used to reawaken the dormant spirit of Europe, by reinforcing the notion of a specifically European narrative existing alongside those of other peoples.

R

Racism, racists

Racism is a pejorative term often used to designate Europeans who oppose obviously harmful political and social tendencies related to immigration. As a blanket term, 'racism' is used to cover everything from single individuals being rude or violent towards minorities, to rational arguments concerning issues such as immigration and ethnicity.

This lack of clarity offers an advantage to those who would defend unreasonable immigration policies, since they, by conflating reasonable arguments and assertions with anti-social behaviour, can prevent the emergence of a rational discussion which they could never win.

This construction of 'racism' and 'racists' also creates an outside group which different elites in society, as well as the radical

Left, can paint as a monstrous Other, to avoid having to take responsibility for their own opinions and actions.

Region, regionalism

A region is a smaller geographical and cultural component of a given territory, often with its own distinct character. Regionalism is the affirmation of such an area and one's own connection to it. As factor creating identity, regionalism is often constructive and enriching, but historically regionalism has also been utilised (much like chauvinist nationalism) by different interest groups to undermine the unity and free political agency of various states.

Right to difference, the

The right to difference is a slogan of GRECE, and the European New Right more broadly, which expresses the importance of defending cultural pluralism, and the specific cultural identity of every people against the homogenising forces of the global marketplace. This differs from multiculturalism in that it asserts the right of all peoples, including the European peoples, to retain their own distinct culture, as opposed to dissolving it into a larger 'melting pot'.

S

Soft genocide

A soft genocide is a genocide accomplished without the use of direct violence. The perpetrators of a soft genocide limit themselves to using metapolitics and legal, political decision-making to reduce birth rates and to bring about the mass immigration of other ethnicities into the territory of the intended victims. While the methods differ from an 'ordinary' genocide, the result and purpose remain the same: to decimate or exterminate the target ethnicity as a group.

Sovereignty

A people or state with the right and ability to act independently and autonomously is said to be sovereign. The term was important after the First World War, when US President Woodrow Wilson sought to dissolve the European and Turkish empires by supporting the development of nation-states in their place.

T

Totalitarianism

In common usage, totalitarianism designates the ideology of a state which exercises unbridled control, authority, and regulation over all the aspects of private and public space in a society. Exactly what constitutes a totalitarian regime depends on which definition is being used. From a liberal perspective, a totalitarian regime is characterised by the absence of formal democracy, human rights, and political liberty in an individualistic sense.

A more in-depth analysis might also examine the degree to which powerful private interests can define the life-world of citizens, and the degree to which individual and collective liberty from the influence of the state bureaucracy, as well as from that of the market and the 'basic values' of society, is possible and actually realised. From this perspective, many Western democracies, in which the values and norms of the mass media permeates the whole of society, and in which the scientifically determined marketing of lifestyles and consumer goods regulates much of the life-world of individuals, can be seen as being just as totalitarian as many societies with a lesser degree of formal political liberty.

Tradition, traditionalism

Traditionalism or the traditional school is a current within the philosophy of comparative religion, which in its current form was first formulated by the French metaphysician René Guénon (1886–1951), and expanded upon by the Italian Julius Evola (1898–1974) and the Swiss Frithjof Schuon (1907–1998), amongst others. It purports to uphold the timeless principles which are in all of the world's ancient religious traditions, which are viewed as manifestations of a single metaphysical source which

underlies reality, thus sharing a common root, esoterically related but differing in exoteric particulars due to differences in
culture, ethnicity, and language. The teachings of the traditional
school are also sometimes referred to, in other permutations, as
perennialism, or as *Sophia Perennis* ('eternal wisdom'). The latter
term has its roots in the Renaissance. The Hindu term *Sanatana
Dharma* — the eternal law — has a similar meaning. From this
perspective, history is seen as a perpetual cycle of ascent and
decline, in which we are currently approaching the bottom of
that cycle, an age marked by corruption and decadence that will
be followed by total destruction. Nevertheless, even in this age
traditionalists hold that it is possible for individuals or small
groups to rise above the decay.

Traditionalism (Catholic)

The Catholic Church has historically been the strongest force
counteracting the revolutionary and modernist forces devas-
tating Europe. This changed drastically following the Second
Vatican Council (1962–1965), when large portions of the Church's
hierarchy revised its doctrines in accordance with revolutionary ideas with the intention of modernising the faith, and thus
helping it to retain its 'relevance' in the modern world. Prior to
the Council, traditionalism was the essential norm within the
Church, and from 1910 until 1967 every Catholic priest was re-
quired to swear the so-called 'oath against modernism'.

After the Council, defenders of Catholic traditionalism came to be known primarily for their defence of the traditional Latin mass, their support for Catholic states, and their opposition to syncretistic and ecumenical tendencies. Catholic traditionalism defends the teaching that the Church was instituted by Christ himself, and that Christ is the only path to salvation.

U

Universalism

Universalism is, among other things, a view of the world in which humanity is represented as a homogeneous whole, one extended family, in which terms such as 'people' and 'identity' lose their relevance.

Universalism is related to egalitarianism, and constitutes a form of the very same political monotheism which lies at the root of all totalitarianisms. According to the universalist mindset, every human being is nothing more than a 'citizen of the world'. Universalist doctrine demands that all cultures should intermix, and thus vanish, since no relevant differences between them exist.

Universalism is a deceitful weapon, useful for every imaginable form of imperialism, including political Islamism and Americanism, since it applies a single model — its own — to the entire world, and claims to aim at the unification of all peoples. It claims that this will bring peace and prosperity to all. In practice, it can only bring about the subordination of all peoples to one single centre of power and interests. Since mankind is, always has been, and always will remain a plurality of unique ethnic groups, with biological and cultural particularities, this form of universalism is always a type of strategy to attain totalitarian dominance of one sort or another.

W

White flight

White flight is a term employed to describe the trend of White people who leave neighbourhoods when the percentage of non-Whites increase. In the United States, White flight has been observed in cities such as Detroit and Atlanta, while Sweden has areas such as Rinkeby, Rosengård, and Hammarkullen, but the phenomenon is common all over the West.

White flight is sometimes viewed by groups critical of immigration as a sort of ongoing organic referendum, in which actions reveals the genuine wishes of the population, more accurately than the votes they cast or even the opinions they express verbally.

Will to Power

The Will to Power (German: *Wille zur Macht*) is a philosophical term, coined by Friedrich Nietzsche in his book, *Thus Spoke Zarathustra*.[9] According to Nietzsche, a quest for power drives man in all his efforts: progress, ambition, self-realisation, personal maturity, the will to reach the highest possible position in life — all these things are the product of the Will to Power.

A common misconception about Nietzsche's philosophy is that the Will to Power must be founded on egotism. In fact, it is wholly possible for a group of individuals to aspire to collective goals through Will to Power. In an unpublished manuscript, *The Will to Power*, Nietzsche writes:

> My idea is that every specific body strives to become master over all space and to extend its force (— its will to power:) and to thrust back all that resists its extension. But it continually encounters similar efforts on the part of other bodies and ends by coming to an arrangement ('union') with those of them that are sufficiently related to it: thus they then conspire together for power. And the process goes on—[10]

---

9 *Thus Spoke Zarathustra: A Book for All and None* (Cambridge: Cambridge University Press, 2006).

10 *The Will to Power*, translated by Walter Kaufmann & R J Hollingdale (New York: Vintage Books, 1968), p. 340.

X

Xenophilia

A xenophile is someone who is or presents himself as being abnormally fond of the Other, and all that is alien or foreign. Xenophilia need not be motivated by sentimentality or emotion, but may just as well be an expression of political or social theatre.

7

Let the Adventure Begin!

Western civilisation can still be saved, and it is a moral duty for every European to strive to accomplish this task. Political activism is both meaningful and necessary.

There are ideologies, politicians, and parties which make the survival of Western civilisation more likely — chief among which may be politicians and parties critical of immigration such as the AfD (*Alternative für Deutschland*), the FPÖ (*Freiheitliche Partei Österreichs*), the Sweden Democrats, or even UKIP — and there are those who make it less so. Never, however, will there be perfect candidates — we must work with what we have. This means supporting the former, with necessary reservations, and opposing the latter. This is a matter of pragmatism, which is a fundamental part of all political success.

Unfortunately, many on the Right choose to withdraw from society and politics because of erroneous, defeatist notions such as that 'nothing can be done'. Often, such people will claim to 'ride the tiger' (a term coined by Evola which advocates waiting out the demise of the modern world until the cycle of history returns to its origin and a new world dawns), since they see opposition to the decay of civilisation as useless. This attitude is often combined with ramblings, usually online, accusing virtually all pro-European politicians for being 'too soft', 'too liberal', or whichever other actual or imagined deficiency of character which, according to the critic in question, makes them unworthy of any support.

This attitude is not always incomprehensible, and criticism of populist politicians with doubtful ideological credentials may well contain grains of truth. Even so, this attitude is always problematic, and it becomes positively repulsive when cynicism and pessimism become political projects in and of themselves. All too many people spend their energy filling up the Internet with extreme, aggressive comments attacking movements and people who want to accomplish positive things, and furthermore have the energy to try.

There is something deeply ugly and self-contradictory in this behaviour. To say that all is lost and nothing can be done, only to simultaneously find some kind of meaning in spending hours behind your keyboard authoring angry outbursts directed against organisations and individuals who actually try to accomplish something positive for the West, makes no sense at all. The least we can expect here is consistency: if the game is lost, it is certainly not any more lost because the True Finns have joined the government coalition in Finland, because the National Front has become the most prominent party in France, or because the Sweden Democrats have reached 25 % support in Swedish opinion polls.

Furthermore: the game is not lost. Even if 'riding the tiger' in the Evolian sense may have been a sound and perhaps necessary strategy during the last half of the last century, this is no longer the case. Europe is bleeding, but the tiger — liberal modernity — is dying as well. It is time to step down from its back and put it out of its misery, while there still is a European civilisation for which to fight.

Raise your heads and do not despair. The struggle for Europe is far from over. It has only just begun. Rather than being depressed about the direction society has taken, view it as an opportunity for an adventure, and as a time when your actions can actually impact history itself.

Being part of the problem or part of the redemption of the Western world is no further away than a change in attitude.

Straighten your back and sweep away all your excuses along with the last shreds of the power of the Left, and let the adventure begin!

Postscript

The War Within

You don't need a PhD to understand that girls and boys are different from one another, or that there are different peoples and cultures. Conversely, you do need one — or several — to be able to construct an explanatory system 'proving' the opposite. As a consequence of the Left's dominance of academia, doing exactly that has succeeded. And the subsequent stuffing of millions of Europeans into state-run 'educational' institutions based on this point of view has had its effect.

What the Left has accomplished is not just the creation of a society marked by cowardice and weakness. It has managed something far more serious; the spiritual amputation of man as such, separating thought and action from each other entirely. The Left has fought a systematic war against our civilisation and culture, but an even more brutal war against mankind itself.

For this reason, you must read and enrich yourself, to learn what it is that is worth defending. This is a prerequisite for being able to orient and arm yourself intellectually. Someone who does not know our principles will sooner or later betray them.

Natural order is deeply rooted in man, and no gender pedagogue of any kind can change this fact. The true Right incarnates this order, and creates a unity of thought and action through it. Accomplishing this is the greatest challenge there is, but also the greatest act of resistance.

You must steel yourself physically and mentally for the turbulent times ahead. All preparation is of course a waste of time unless you are ready to subordinate yourself to a principle — our fight is not a cosy pastime during which you get to admire your own intellectualism.

Begin by throwing out your TV, sit down, and figure out where you stand. Do you think the family is central to our survival? Then it is time to start embodying this conviction. You must get married, have children, affirm gender roles, and be faithful to your significant other. Finding the spouse of your dreams may not be easy in this decadent time, but you must stand firm in your ambition to do so. You must distance yourself from the type of life in which family does not matter. This means rejecting not only abortion, one-night stands, and pornography, but also serial monogamy. Marital loyalty is for life.

Too harsh, old fashioned, and boring? You don't feel like it? Then you are half a man who won't integrate thought and action into a whole. Do not forget the proverb that it is absurd that a man should rule others, who cannot rule himself — it applies to you as well. You, through your own life and action, decide if the principles of the Right will be victorious.

> 'For if you are living according to the flesh, you must die; but if by the Spirit you are putting to death the deeds of the body, you will live.' (Romans 8:13)

The war begins within you!

BJÖRN HERSTAD
Businessman & Entrepreneur

OTHER BOOKS FROM ARKTOS

Sri Dharma Pravartaka Acharya	*The Dharma Manifesto*
Alain de Benoist	*Beyond Human Rights*
	Carl Schmitt Today
	Manifesto for a European Renaissance
	On the Brink of the Abyss
	The Problem of Democracy
Arthur Moeller van den Bruck	*Germany's Third Empire*
Kerry Bolton	*Revolution from Above*
Alexander Dugin	*Eurasian Mission: An Introduction to Neo-Eurasianism*
	The Fourth Political Theory
	Last War of the World-Island
	Putin vs Putin
Koenraad Elst	*Return of the Swastika*
Julius Evola	*Fascism Viewed from the Right*
	Metaphysics of War
	Notes on the Third Reich
	The Path of Cinnabar
	A Traditionalist Confronts Fascism
Guillaume Faye	*Archeofuturism*
	Convergence of Catastrophes
	Sex and Deviance
	Why We Fight
Daniel S. Forrest	*Suprahumanism*
Andrew Fraser	*The WASP Question*
Génération Identitaire	*We are Generation Identity*

OTHER BOOKS FROM ARKTOS

OTHER BOOKS FROM ARKTOS

RICHARD RUDGLEY

Barbarians

Essential Substances

Wildest Dreams

ERNST VON SALOMON

It Cannot Be Stormed

The Outlaws

TROY SOUTHGATE

Tradition & Revolution

OSWALD SPENGLER

Man and Technics

TOMISLAV SUNIC

Against Democracy and Equality

ABIR TAHA

Defining Terrorism: The End of Double Standards

Nietzsche's Coming God, or the Redemption of the Divine

Verses of Light

BAL GANGADHAR TILAK

The Arctic Home in the Vedas

DOMINIQUE VENNER

The Shock of History: Religion, Memory, Identity

MARKUS WILLINGER

A Europe of Nations

Generation Identity

DAVID J. WINGFIELD (ED.)

The Initiate: Journal of Traditional Studies

CPSIA information can be obtained
at www.ICGtesting.com
Printed in the USA
BVOW00s0306031216
469630BV00003B/132/P